SEARCH
FOR THE Beloved
Community

SEARCH
FOR THE **Beloved Community**

The Thinking of
Martin Luther King Jr.

KENNETH L. SMITH

—— *and* ——

IRA G. ZEPP JR.

JUDSON PRESS ® VALLEY FORGE

Library of Congress Cataloging-in-Publication Data

Smith, Kenneth L., 1925-
    Search for the beloved community :
    the thinking of Martin Luther King Jr. / Kenneth L. Smith, Ira G. Zepp, Jr.
        p.   cm.
    Includes bibliographical references and index.
    ISBN 0-8170-1282-6 (alk. paper)
    1. King, Martin Luther, Jr., 1929-1968 – Political and social views.
    2. King, Martin Luther, Jr., 1929-1968 – Sources. I. Zepp, Ira G. II. Title.
E185.97.K5S58 1998
323'.092–dc21   97-52278

Printed in the U.S.A.

06   05   04   03   02   01   99   98
10   9   8   7   6   5   4   3   2   1

To our wives,
Mary
and
Esther,
with love and gratitude

I would like this third printing of *Search for the Beloved Community* to honor the life and work of Kenneth L. Smith (affectionately known as "Snuffy"), who taught Christian social ethics at Crozer Theological Seminary both in Chester, Pennsylvania, and in Rochester, New York, and where, in 1951, Martin Luther King Jr. was Smith's student. Smith contributed much to the original publication of this book and joyfully and proudly celebrated King's embodiment of Christian praxis.

IGZ

"Have we, in America, had a hero in our time — that is, since World War II? I can think of only one man with a serious claim, Martin Luther King. The theme was high, the occasion noble, the stage open to the world's eye, the courage clear and against odds. And martyrdom came to purge all dross away. King seems made for the folk consciousness, and the folk consciousness is the Valhalla of the true hero — not the gossip column. King may even, someday, enter into the folk consciousness of the white world, which may yet underlie, at what depth it is hard to guess, the Culture of Blab."*

*Robert Penn Warren, "A Dearth of Heroes," *American Heritage* vol. 23 (October 1972), p. 99, © Robert Penn Warren.

Contents

Foreword

THE FIRST EDITION of this book appeared in 1974. A year earlier, Kenneth L. Smith, who co-authored it with Ira G. Zepp Jr., had taught what turned out to be the only course I would take as a student on Martin Luther King Jr. As I studied with Smith at Colgate Rochester Divinity School/Bexley Hall/ Crozer Theological Seminary, I was introduced to much of the content of *Search for the Beloved Community* before it actually appeared in published form. It was clear to me, even then, that Smith and Zepp were charting a new course in King scholarship, and that their book would have lasting value. This view is confirmed in some measure by Judson Press's decision to reprint the book nearly twenty-five years later.

This volume was the first highly sophisticated treatment of King's intellectual sources and categories. Its focus extends beyond Mohandas K. Gandhi to a serious consideration of Christian theology and ethics, which, in Smith's and Zepp's estimation, structured King's personal religious faith and grounded both his concern for social justice and his nonviolent strategy. This position finds some reinforcement in more recent examinations of King's intellectual life by John J. Ansbro, Ervin Smith, William D. Watley, Garth Baker-Fletcher, and others.

Smith and Zepp render an analysis that points to several conclusions. First, that King's intellectual pilgrimage began at the predominantly black Morehouse College in Atlanta, Georgia in the mid-1940s. This point is more commonly accepted and treated by King scholars today than it was when *Search for the Beloved Community* first appeared. This is important because what King inherited in terms of ideas and values from George D.

Kelsey, Benjamin E. Mays, and other African-American preacher-intellectuals at Morehouse prepared him for the academic challenges that later confronted him in seminary and graduate school.

The second conclusion is that a major shift occurred in King's intellectual pilgrimage as his ideas reached high levels of refinement and maturity at Crozer Theological Seminary and Boston University in the late 1940s and early 1950s. Such a conclusion is irrefutable, especially since Crozer and Boston provided the contexts for King's serious intellectual quest for a method to challenge and ultimately eliminate social evil. Smith and Zepp develop this point with considerable analytical depth and clarity.

Another conclusion is that King's theology and ethics had definite historical and intellectual sources. Of particular importance in this regard are Protestant liberalism and personal idealism, though Smith and Zepp also devote attention to Niebuhrian Christian realism and Gandhian nonviolence and civil disobedience. The scholarship over the last two decades lends support to Smith's and Zepp's claims regarding King's tremendous indebtedness to Protestant liberalism and personal idealism, but there is a more conscious recognition today of how King interpreted and appropriated these streams in light of the teachings and traditions of the black church.

Yet another conclusion is that King's intellectual quest cannot be divorced in any way from his work as a social activist. Indeed, he represented "the intellectual-activist type" that had constituted the principal model for W. E. B. Du Bois's theory of the "Talented Tenth" years earlier. In this sense, King broke with that side of the Western intellectual tradition that separates the *intellectual* from the *social,* and which prevents intellectuals from committing themselves unselfishly to the uplifting of the poor and the oppressed. For King, this dichotomy between the *intellectual* and the *practical* never really existed, despite the view that he was not socially and politically involved prior to the mid-1950s. Having grown up in an African-American community, with much exposure to the extended family, the black church, and a black college environment, and where men were expected to succeed despite segregation and to become leaders in the struggle for freedom, King was not likely to be a detached intellectual who confined himself to the articulation of abstract, complicated ideas. His view that the collective intellect should be put to the service of human liberation, and that ideas find meaning only when translated into practical action, became the driving force in his efforts to achieve the Beloved Community. Smith and Zepp pioneered among King scholars in giving proper emphasis to this point.

Search for the Beloved Community, by some standards, remains the best intellectual biography of King. In more precise terms, it testifies to the fact that King was not only an outstanding social activist who contributed enormously to the improvement of the human condition, but was also a polished intellectual who challenged and influenced the world through the power of ideas.

Lewis V. Baldwin
Vanderbilt University
Nashville, Tennessee

Preface to the Third Printing

I AM SURE I SPEAK for my departed good friend and co-author, Kenneth L. Smith, when I say how rewarding it is to have *Search for the Beloved Community: The Thinking of Martin Luther King Jr.* reprinted after nearly twenty-five years.

Our attempt in this book was a relatively modest one — to flesh out the autobiographical journey King outlined in the several versions of his famous essay "Pilgrimage to Non-Violence," found in *Stride Toward Freedom, Strength to Love* and in *The Christian Century* (April 13, 1960). In this confession, a kind of *apologia*, what he called his "intellectual odyssey," King recounts in some detail the scholars and books he claimed influenced his thinking. It is these sources we trace, analyze, and discuss in detail.

Our project was also a relatively limited one. An intellectual biography is never a complete biography. We anticipated this criticism in the introduction (p. 5) by clearly stating that King's life and thought could not be reduced to intellectual sources and that his black middle-class family, the black Baptist church, his friends and advisers were indispensable to his spiritual and intellectual formation. Because of our own limitations, we intentionally confined our study to those written texts that, by King's own admission, obviously made a significant impact on his thought.

There is no question that King's evangelical liberal Christianity was deeply affected by his black church heritage, which was the heart of the man. It is what we in religious studies call the "prestige of the beginnings." And it is now our great good fortune that this "heart" has been brilliantly delineated by several King scholars over the last decade and a half. Notable among these is

James Cone in an essay entitled "Martin Luther King, Jr.: Black Theology — Black Church," written for *Theology Today* (January 1984). Here Cone speaks of King's "primary commitment being determined by the Black Church community."

More complete and compelling studies, however, are Lewis Baldwin's two books (*There Is a Balm in Gilead* and *To Make the Wounded Whole*), which clearly and systematically outline the impact of the black church, family, and culture on the life and thought of King. This scholarship was desperately needed and more than adequately rounds out the dominant influences on King's thinking.

Nevertheless, Smith and I very much appreciated the positive and helpfully critical response to this first serious study of King's thought and the account of how he wove together a network of various theological traditions in the name of the black freedom struggle. Martin King invoked unself-consciously observable intellectual sources of his thought and freely and gratefully acknowledged indebtedness to them, e.g., evangelical liberalism, the social gospel, personalism, and Gandhi's nonviolent methods with all the foregoing, to a degree, qualified by Reinhold Niebuhr's Christian realism.

Ten years of intellectual training may not have provided his *esse*, but they became his *bene esse*. It provided him with conceptual tools to articulate his critique of an acculturated Christianity and his vision of the Beloved Community. An example of his first-rate Christian mind and his ability to creatively broker the Western theological heritage is his *Letter from Birmingham Jail*, one of the finest pieces of twentieth-century American Christian literature.

The masterful job King did with these mostly Euro-American texts in designing a theology to free his people was a precursor of black liberation theology led by James Cone, J. Deotis Roberts, Vincent Harding, and Major Jones.

This book also inadvertently anticipated the plagiarism issue which has occupied King scholars for the past decade. We note that on five occasions King did not properly credit references to

Gandhi, Paul Tillich, Reinhold Niebuhr, Paul Ramsey, and Anders Nygren. It was our opinion that the hectic and harried pace of King's life naturally precluded precise attention to footnoting all of his sources. We also believed that there was no intention on King's part to mislead the reader and that whatever ghostwriting went on reflected the spirit, if not the letter, of King's thought. In the early 1970s, as well, we did not have the benefit of the scrutiny of King's written material which appeared fifteen years later. Since our book was first published, David Garrow's *Bearing the Cross* and Keith Miller's *Voice of Deliverance* have analyzed carefully the plagiarism and ghostwriting issues and the reader is invited to consult these books for additional helpful critical analysis.

However, the editor and I have agreed to reprint the book as it originally appeared. We do this out of deference to Kenneth Smith and with a belief that the book is still a valuable academic period piece. Smith and I were concerned with King's written sources, attributed and otherwise, and his unique brokerage of the ideas issuing from them.

So the thesis of our book remains. While King powerfully lived his Christianity and deeply felt his faith, he also knew that Christianity could be thought as well as felt and lived. We know he was a great preacher and orator and an effective Christian social activist for civil rights. We must keep being reminded that King, in his own way, was also an important theologian.

Ira G. Zepp Jr.
Professor Emeritus of Religious Studies
Western Maryland College

October 1997

Acknowledgments

I wish especially to thank three former teachers: Dr. Charles Crain of Western Maryland College, who introduced me to the study of religion; the late Dr. Carl Michalson of Drew Theological Seminary, who made theology live and breathe; and Dr. John Cronin, S.S., of St. Mary's Seminary and University in Baltimore, who patiently guided me through my doctoral dissertation research. I owe these men an immense debt of gratitude.

IRA G. ZEPP JR.

I am indebted to too many people to cite any individuals in particular. I owe more than words can express to my teachers at the University of Richmond, Crozer Theological Seminary, and The Divinity School of Duke University. A special word of thanks is due Ms. Doris Griffith who read the manuscript and offered invaluable suggestions about grammar and style.

KENNETH L. SMITH

Introduction

MARTIN LUTHER KING JR. is well known as a civil rights activist who employed nonviolent resistance as the method of achieving social justice for the black population of the United States. It is not so well known that both his concern for social justice and his nonviolent strategy were rooted in Christian theology and ethics, and that he was sustained throughout his career by a deeply personal religious faith, including a firm belief in a personal God.

Most of the studies of Martin Luther King thus far have attributed a major significance to the influence of Mahatma Gandhi upon King's thought and have ignored almost entirely the distinctly Christian roots of King's theology and ethics. To whatever degree King may have been influenced by non-Christian sources, such as Gandhi, whose influence will not be minimized herein, it remains true that King's "intellectual" categories were drawn from Christian theology and ethics. King's interpreters have not understood that many of the concepts attributed to Gandhi were actually cardinal tenets of the school of Christian theology and ethics which had the most influence upon King's thought.

As black theology has become popular and as we have been made aware of African religion and philosophy by experts, we have learned that a hallmark of African religious experience has been its optimism and a faith in the justice of the universe. Such a faith illustrates, according to J. S. Mbiti in *African Religions and Philosophy*, the resiliency of African religious life under extreme pressures and adverse conditions. Some have been quick to note, therefore, that the source of King's optimism and hope was his cultural heritage as an African American. While this point is well taken, the fact remains that King's "intellectual" categories were not those of African religion and philosophy. His conception of hope was expressed in terms of the Christian doctrine of the kingdom of God. He accepted the love ethic of Jesus as one of his basic principles, and his optimism was rooted in his belief that humanity's natural inclination to altruism could always be appealed to with positive results. Both of these tenets were the heritage of Protestant liberalism.

Emphasis on the role of a civil rights activist, Gandhi's influence, and African-American culture has tended to obscure King's debt to Christian theology and ethics except for the studies by a few interpreters. "King was regarded," Herbert Richardson has written, "as a civil rights leader and as a man of extraordinary personal valor, but he has not been understood as a brilliant and mature theologian: the first two would, however, have been impossible without the third."[1] Daniel Day Williams, speaking specifically of nonviolent resistance, agrees that "purely sociological or political interpretations of this movement will misunderstand it."[2] Even some, who have little, if any, interest in King's theology and ethics, have been forced to admit: "There was never any doubt of Martin's belief in the basic tenets of the Christian propositions on which he stood."[3]

But we do not have to depend upon secondhand interpretations to show the importance of Christian theology and ethics for King; we have his own testimony regarding what he called his "pilgrimage to nonviolence."[4] In a speech to the National Conference on Religion and Race in 1963, King said:

> I am happy to say that the nonviolent movement in America has come not from secular forces but from the heart of the Negro church.... The great principles of love and justice which stand at the center of the nonviolent movement are deeply rooted in our Judeo-Christian heritage.[5]

Martin Luther King's theology and ethics did not develop "from scratch" or in a vacuum. They had very definite historical and intellectual sources; chief among these were Protestant liberalism and the philosophy of personalism.[6] The liberalizing process began at Morehouse College with George Kelsey's Bible course and Benjamin May's preaching, waxed strong at Crozer Seminary under the liberalism of George W. Davis, and matured at Boston with the personalism of Edgar S. Brightman and L. Harold DeWolf. "Golden Day" is the title L. D. Reddick aptly used in *Crusader Without Violence*,[7] the first of the biographies based largely upon extensive personal interviews with King, to describe King's theological studies at Crozer Seminary and Boston University.

The experience with Kelsey and May apparently persuaded King finally to choose the Christian ministry as a vocation instead of a career in medicine or law. However, the story of King's intellectual pilgrimage at Morehouse College has been told as fully as possible at this time.[8] At any rate, we have King's own testimony that he began to articulate his theology and ethics and to make a "serious intellectual quest for a method to eliminate social evil"[9] while a student at Crozer Theological Seminary. There were undoubtedly multiple reasons why King would embark upon such a quest, but none was more important than the one stated in his application to Crozer in the spring of 1948, wherein he writes of "an inescapable urge to serve society" and "a sense of responsibility which I could not escape."[10]

Although King had been reared in the fundamentalist, simplistic piety of black Baptist Protestantism in the South, a fact which almost dissuaded him from entering the ministry, he was introduced in his undergraduate studies at Morehouse College and later in his graduate studies at Crozer Seminary to theological liberalism. In a speech before the American Baptist Convention, shortly after the Montgomery bus boycott had been completed, King publicly stated:

> I gained my major influences from . . . Morehouse and Crozer —
> and I feel greatly indebted to them. They gave me the basic truths
> I now believe . . . the world view which . . . I have . . . the idea of
> the oneness of humanity and the dignity and worth of all human

personality.... At Crozer I found the actual living out of Christian beliefs.[11]

King would continue his intellectual quest at Boston University's School of Theology where the geographical locale was different but the theological climate was quite similar. A study of the books written about King thus far reveals that their authors have at best only a superficial knowledge of the intellectual sources of King's thought.[12] Some of them have indeed given valuable treatments of the Morehouse years. All of them include the fact that King earned the Bachelor of Divinity degree at Crozer and the Doctor of Philosophy degree at Boston. In addition, they mention some of the best-known influences, such as Walter Rauschenbusch, Mahatma Gandhi, Reinhold Niebuhr, and Edgar S. Brightman. But none of them goes beyond King's own accounts of his pilgrimage and the limited material of Reddick's *Crusader Without Violence*. None of them deals in depth, either historically or analytically, with the intellectual sources, the people and movements essential to a thorough understanding of King's thought. Since King did not write a systematic theology, it is absolutely essential to go to the springs from which he drank to comprehend what he was trying to affirm.

Inadequate research on the intellectual sources of King's thought has led to some monumental blunders, to say the least. One author attributes a great deal of significance to the Methodist influence of the School of Theology of Boston University, although King had received degrees from two Baptist schools (Morehouse College and Crozer Seminary) before studying at Boston.[13] Another has failed to realize that the study of Walter Rauschenbusch was a definite part of King's seminary curriculum as were the life and works of Gandhi.[14] Still another falsely assumes that King took a special course at Crozer on the Old Testament prophets.[15] But there was no regular required course on the Hebrew prophets, and King never took the elective course taught periodically on that subject.

What seem to be the reasons for such glaring mistakes in the heretofore published volumes on Martin Luther King? There are two major reasons: insufficient research and inadequate knowledge of Christian theology and ethics, notably certain ideas and concepts prevalent in twentieth-century liberal Protestant theology and ethics. For all of King's biographers to date, information about the intellectual sources of his thought has been sketchy at best; the scholars and movements mentioned have been little more than well-known names. The serious limitations of the treatments of King's intellectual sources have led the authors, in the interest of historical accuracy as well as whatever constructive insights might be thrown upon King's theology and ethics, to attempt to reconstruct that part of the record.

The authors feel that they are in a better position to discuss the intellectual sources of King's thought than the facile and quick treatments by the heretofore published biographers. One of the authors (Zepp) wrote his doctoral dissertation on the intellectual sources of King's thought. The dissertation was based upon an extensive study of not only King's books and articles but also the unpublished materials in the Boston Collection.[16] The other author (Smith), having received his Bachelor of Divinity degree at Crozer Seminary in June, 1948, was privileged to have taught King at Crozer during King's senior year (1950–1951). King's professors at Crozer had also been Smith's instructors; many of the courses King took at Crozer had also been taken by Smith only a few years earlier. Both the professors of those courses and their content are still remembered with much nostalgia.

This work is clearly and intentionally an "intellectual" biography. The authors are fully cognizant of the fact that the life and career of Martin Luther King, like any other eminent personality, cannot be accounted for solely in terms of the influence of professors, books, and theological and ethical theories. There were naturally other influences which shaped his attitudes and behavior; chief among these were his black, middle-class family, the religion of the black Baptist church, his friends and advisers, and the patterns of racial segregation and discrimination. A good case could be made for the assertion that King's policy decisions from the outset were influenced as much by events as by theological and ethical presuppositions. The evidence suggests, to cite one example, that King did not fully embrace the tenets and implications of nonviolent resistance until *after* the Montgomery bus boycott and his trip to India.[17] Events had a significant influence upon King's change in tactics after Chicago. He candidly admitted that events raised many intellectual problems for him that remained unresolved at the time of his death. Although it is impossible to draw a firm line between intellectual influences and those of family, religion, and personal relationships, it is clear, nevertheless, that King was indebted to many people and movements of nineteenth- and twentieth-century theology and philosophy. We have limited our study to those scholars and schools of thought that obviously made a significant impact upon King's thought.

In order to understand the intellectual sources of King's thought, it is necessary to understand his experience at Crozer Seminary because there he began to make "a serious intellectual quest for a method to eliminate social evil...." When Martin Luther King Jr. arrived at Crozer Theological Seminary in Chester, Pennsylvania, in the fall of 1948 at the age of nineteen, he encountered both a social milieu and a theological climate of opinion quite different from anything he had heretofore experienced. On the social side, the situation raised considerably his anxiety level. Whereas he had lived at home while attending Morehouse College and whereas Morehouse had been an all-black school with an all-black faculty, now he found himself over six hundred miles away from family and friends (except Walter McCall) and only one of a few blacks among a student body of about fifty students taught by an all-white faculty. His description of his feelings and reactions are so frank and revealing that they warrant recording.

> I was well aware of the typical white stereotype of the Negro, that he is always late, that he's loud and always laughing, that he's dirty and messy, and for a while I was terribly conscious of trying to avoid identification with it. If I were a minute late to

class, I was almost morbidly conscious of it and sure that everyone else noticed it. Rather than be thought of as always laughing, I'm afraid I was grimly serious for a time. I had a tendency to overdress, to keep my room spotless, my shoes perfectly shined and my clothes immaculately pressed....[18]

The theological climate was equally as disturbing as the social milieu. Crozer Seminary was widely known for its liberal theological stance and high academic standards, so much so that it was often referred to as "the little University of Chicago Divinity School." Liberalism was still in its heyday, and *The Crozer Quarterly* was one of the best-known liberal theological journals in the United States. All of the newer faculty members had been trained in seminaries where liberalism had become the dominant approach to theology and Scripture. Therefore, a tradition took shape at Crozer which was strongly influenced by the American religious liberalism that had arisen as a reaction to the rigid orthodoxy of nineteenth-century Calvinism. The liberal tradition would survive, largely unchallenged, until the early years of the decade of the 1950s.

The faculty had been influenced by the attempts of the so-called new theology of the late nineteenth and early twentieth centuries to come to grips not only with biblical criticism but also with the Darwinian evolutionary hypothesis, the advances of the natural and social sciences, and the emerging technology of the Industrial Revolution. The faculty had accepted for about a quarter of a century the position that the obscurantism of orthodoxy (i.e., fundamentalism) rendered Christianity ill-prepared to deal with the "modern mind" and "the spirit of the age." To this end, they advocated a liberal theology which appealed, on the one hand, to reason as an accommodation to the scientific method and, on the other hand, to religious experience as a reaction to doctrinal orthodoxy. Such emphases had led to a historical approach to Christian doctrine. The appropriation of biblical criticism had placed both dogma and Scripture in a perspective that disallowed a belief in either verbal inspiration or the sanctity of creeds and confessions. On the positive side, the history of the

Bible, the life of Jesus, and the history of Christian doctrines had become important disciplines.[19]

The prominence accorded higher criticism was manifested in the fact that during King's first year of study at Crozer about two-thirds of the total course load was devoted to two double majors (i.e., eight quarter hours each): an "Introduction to the Old Testament," taught by James B. Pritchard,[20] and "The History and Literature of the New Testament," taught by Morton Scott Enslin.[21] It is true that King "found Professor Morton Scott Enslin's liberal interpretation of the New Testament fascinating," because that had been the case for two generations of students before him. Enslin was a brilliant New Testament and Greek scholar, and every student who had studied with him and had taken him seriously had been profoundly indebted to him. King was no exception, but not in the sense indicated by one of his biographers. The conclusion, for example, drawn by William R. Miller is patently absurd, revealing a complete lack of knowledge of either King's "theological basis" and "perspective on society" or Enslin's, or both.

> During his first semester, Martin...found a theological basis for the perspective on society which had been evolving from his own experiences, and one which accorded well with Enslin's biblical views. Walter Rauschenbusch's *Christianity and the Social Crisis* provided the key.[22]

The theological and biblical views of Morton Scott Enslin were diametrically opposed to those of Walter Rauschenbusch. Rauschenbusch, whom we shall discuss at some length in chapter 2, had been an exponent of the "liberal Jesus" school of thought, and he had advanced a socio-ethical interpretation of theology. Jesus had been conceived as the prophet of a new righteousness. The central tenet of his teaching had been the kingdom of God, conceived as an ideal social order to be the result of the gradual Christianization of the individual and society by the ethic of love. Jesus was viewed as the moral example all people should and could emulate.

Morton Scott Enslin's views, by way of contrast, had been significantly influenced by Albert Schweitzer, who had focused attention upon the eschatological elements in Jesus' thought with such vigor and critical acumen about the turn of the twentieth century in *The Quest of the Historical Jesus* that the search for the "historical Jesus" appeared to many New Testament scholars to have come to an abrupt end.[23] Enslin agreed with Schweitzer that the expectation of an imminent, catastrophic establishment of the kingdom had been central in Jesus' teaching. Hence, to those liberals, like Rauschenbusch, who had been basing their theology upon the discovery of the historical Jesus, the emphasis upon eschatology came as a rude shock.

Since Schweitzer accepted the view that for Jesus the kingdom of God had been eschatological in character, a crucial question was raised in his mind regarding the permanent validity of the ethics of Jesus. If the eschatological interpretation were correct, it now appeared that the impending kingdom had provided the sanction for moral renewal. This being the case, Jesus' ethical teachings had been relevant only for the critical interim between the proclamation and the actualization of the kingdom. But the kingdom did not materialize; not only had it not come "within the generation," but it also had not appeared after two thousand years. On these grounds, Schweitzer concluded that Jesus' ethic should be viewed as an "interim ethic" with no meaning for modern people. Since Jesus' ethic had been predicated upon a misconception, it would be futile to cite his teachings as norms for a modern ethic.

Morton Scott Enslin, whom Miller cites as crucial for King, followed the views of Schweitzer very closely.[24] But it would be difficult to find a position farther removed from the thought of Schweitzer and Enslin than King's position. King was an exponent of the "liberal Jesus" school of thought, and that appeal of Jesus is best expressed in the Sermon on the Mount. Speaking of the Montgomery bus boycott, King wrote:

> ...in the first days of the protest...the phrase most often heard
> was "Christian love." It was the Sermon on the Mount, rather

than a doctrine of passive resistance, that initially inspired the Negroes of Montgomery to dignified social action. It was Jesus of Nazareth that stirred the Negroes to protest with the creative weapon of love.[25]

Although there was more to King's position, a "Jesus monism" is evident in his thought similar to that found in Charles Sheldon's famous tract In His Steps and in whose mind the primary ethical question had been, "What would Jesus do?" But this approach had been often derided publicly by Enslin as "pious hogwash." Enslin was vehemently opposed to attempts to draw up blueprints for social and political life.

The writers submit that for Miller to attribute a major influence to Dr. Enslin upon King at the points indicated is irresponsible scholarship, leading to a perversion of the intellectual sources of King's theology and ethics, and they are confident that Dr. Enslin would be the first to agree. (Needless to say, this is the kind of research on the intellectual sources of King's thought which the authors have set out to correct.) Since this interpretation of the influence of Enslin upon King does not appear in Reddick, the only information in Miller's account of King's studies at Crozer which does not come from that source, we assume that Miller manufactured it out of thin air.

L. D. Reddick is closer to the truth about Enslin's influence upon King when he comments upon King's observation, "Enslin was one of those precise scholars and superb linguists, who had a rather iconoclastic manner of criticism."

> Professor Enslin's course on the New Testament was so shocking that the fundamentalist beliefs of some of his students were completely uprooted.... Enslin was always the unperturbed scholar — accurate and relentlessly logical. He did for Martin what Kant said Hume did for him: "He knocked me out of my dogmatic slumber."[26]

Nevertheless, one should not infer from this testimony to Enslin that King accepted Enslin's biblical and theological views. It meant rather that (1) he could no longer be a fundamentalist and a biblicist, and (2) he had to look elsewhere for a theological basis for his beliefs about ethics and society already growing from his own experiences as a black man in the South and from his studies at Morehouse College.

This was, in brief, the theological climate of opinion into which King came to begin his theological studies, and his first theological and ethical formulations were hammered out within this context. The alternatives presented, generally speaking, were either fundamentalism or liberalism. To be sure, many varieties of liberalism were represented on the faculty, but the major argument took place between the "modernistic" liberalism (i.e., humanism and/or naturalism) of the biblical and historical departments and the "evangelical liberalism"* of George W. Davis, Professor of Christian Theology. Davis was a dynamic embodiment of evangelical liberalism at its very best, and he rescued many students, including Martin Luther King, from the extremes of fundamentalism, on the one side, and humanism, on the other side. Some students, of course, did go all the way over to humanism in their revolt against fundamentalism, but King never went that far in his revolt, and it was the kind of liberalism represented by George W. Davis which made the difference. This is why King said in a letter to Davis while a student at Boston University: "I must admit that my theological and philosophical studies with you [Davis] have been of tremendous help to me in my present studies. In the most decisive moments, I find your influence creeping through."[27]

---

*Since frequent references will be made to "evangelical liberalism" in regard to Davis to distinguish him from "modernistic liberalism," the distinction made between these two terms by Kenneth Cauthen in The Impact of American Religious Liberalism (New York: Harper & Row, Publishers, 1962) should be called to the attention of the reader at this point: "The evangelical liberals can appropriately be thought of as 'serious Christians' who were searching for a theology which could be believed by 'intelligent moderns.' They stood squarely within the Christian tradition and accepted as normative for their thinking what they understood to be the essence of historical Christianity....The modernistic liberals can best be thought of as 'intelligent moderns' who nevertheless wished to be thought of as 'serious Christians' in some real sense....They believed there were elements of permanent significance in the Christian tradition which ought to be retained. However, the standard by which the abiding values of the Christianity of the past were to be measured was derived from the presuppositions of modern science, philosophy, psychology, and social thought" (pp. 27, 29).

CHAPTER ONE

George W. Davis
and Evangelical Liberalism

MARTIN LUTHER KING very clearly found some of the answers he had been searching for in the thought of Walter Rauschenbusch. His introduction to Rauschenbusch took place in an elective course with Dr. George Washington Davis, Professor of Christian Theology at Crozer Seminary. Although theology was not required during the first year of study, King elected two courses with Davis called "Great Theologians" and "Christian Mysticism"[1] during the second and third terms respectively because his major interest was in the fields of theology and philosophy.[2] Walter Rauschenbusch, a key figure for Davis, and for King, was one of the major figures covered in some detail in the "Great Theologians" course.

At the outset, Davis struck a responsive nerve in King, both as a teacher and as a person. "He was," King later told Reddick, "a marvelous teacher, conversant with the trends of modern culture and yet sincerely religious. He was warm and Christian. It was easy to get close to him."[3] The feeling was mutual because Davis also had a very high regard for King. In a report to the Placement Committee, Davis's assessment contained these phrases:

> 1. Exceptional intellectual ability — discriminating mind; 2. Very personable; 3. Makes good impression in public speaking and discussion.... Good speaking voice; 4. A man of high character; 5. Should make an excellent minister or teacher. He has the mind for the latter.[4]

The high regard King had for Davis is shown in the fact that out of a total of one hundred and ten quarter hours required for the Bachelor of Divinity degree, King took thirty-four of them, mostly electives, with Davis in courses on systematic and historical theology, philosophy and psychology of religion, and comparative religion. In these courses, King studied not only Rauschenbusch, but also other noted theologians like William Newton Clarke and William Adams Brown; philosophers of religion like William E. Hocking, D. C. Macintosh, and Edgar S. Brightman; psychologists of religion like William James and James B. Pratt; and mystics like Rufus Jones and Douglas Steere. Davis was an interesting blend of the evangelical liberalism of Clarke and Brown, the empiricism of Macintosh, the personalism of Brightman, and the mysticism of Jones. A combination of these strands of thought was common among liberals in the twenties, thirties, and forties.

Students who took a wide range of courses with Davis were introduced in some depth to the history and systematic formulations of both liberal theology and philosophy of religion. King was no exception, and the major themes of both disciplines would find their way into his theology and ethics at key points. King inherited from Davis the best of the liberal tradition — Friedrich S. Schleiermacher, Albrecht R. Ritschl, Horace Bushnell, William Newton Clarke, Walter Rauschenbusch, Edgar S. Brightman, and a host of others. Davis was a pivotal figure in King's intellectual pilgrimage, and it is impossible to understand the intellectual sources and the intellectual categories of King's thought without a thorough knowledge of George Washington Davis and the place he occupied on the Crozer Seminary faculty between 1938 and 1960.

George Washington Davis (1902–1960) decided early in his life to enter the Christian ministry and to serve in a parish setting. As a native of Pittsburgh, Pennsylvania, he attended the public schools there, and he pursued his undergraduate studies at the University of Pittsburgh earning the Bachelor of Arts degree in 1924. When the time came to begin his theological studies, he selected Rochester Theological Seminary (B.D., 1928; Th.M., 1929), a Baptist institution in Rochester, New York, noted for its liberal theological and social stance largely because of the fact that Walter Rauschenbusch had taught there from 1897 to 1918. Davis had been attracted to the liberal social stances of the school because he had been influenced significantly by his father, who had been active in the trade union movement in the steel mills of Pittsburgh.

While at Rochester Theological Seminary (later Colgate Rochester Divinity School and now Colgate Rochester/Bexley Hall/Crozer Seminary), Davis decided upon a teaching career, and after graduation he entered the Divinity School of Yale University (Ph.D., 1932) where his major professor had been D. C. Macintosh, the internationally known and respected "empirical" theologian and pacifist. Before accepting the chair of Christian Theology at Crozer Seminary in 1938, Davis served as pastor of churches in Calais, Maine, and Columbus, Ohio. By the time he arrived at Crozer to teach in 1938, he was admirably equipped to carry on the liberal tradition of Clarke and the social gospel of Walter Rauschenbusch, and his lectures, delivered with passion and enthusiasm, bore the indelible stamp of both.

Martin Luther King took the required work in systematic theology with Davis during the first and second terms of King's second year at Crozer (1949–1950). During the second term of that year, he also took one of Davis's electives, "The Development of Christian Ideas,"[5] which, as manifested in the text used, the two-volume work on *A History of Christian Thought* by A. C. McGiffert, presented a liberal interpretation of the history of Christian doctrine in the tradition of Adolph Harnack. The required course, called "Christian Theology for Today," gave a similar interpretation of systematic theology. The course was a study of

> the Nature and method of theology; the Christian faith in its systematic formulations; the Christian conception of God; man, his nature, need, and destiny; the religious significance of Jesus of Nazareth and his part in salvation; the place and task of the Church as the carrier of the Christian faith and experience.[6]

The degree of Davis's attachment to evangelical liberalism is evident in the textbooks required: William Newton Clarke's *An Outline of Christian Theology*[7] and William Adams Brown's *Christian Theology in Outline.*[8] Each student was required to submit a detailed outline of those texts as the major assignment of the course. Davis's lectures in methodology and content paralleled the texts very closely. The volumes of Clarke and Brown were classical texts in the liberal tradition, and both authors had served as theological mentors to a whole generation of liberals like George W. Davis. They also served as King's mentors as their thought was studied from their books and interpreted by Davis's lectures.

The texts of Clarke and Brown were closely argued systematic treatises taking Jesus, Scripture, history, and reason with utmost seriousness. Brown had been influenced by Ritschl, and Clarke's emphasis upon religious experience revealed a debt to Schleiermacher. This influence is seen in the first two sentences of Clarke's *Outline* in which he defined the task of theology: "Theology is preceded by religion, as botany by the life of plants. Religion is the reality of which theology is the study."[9] "Theology is the fruit of religion, and religion is a life."[10] This note, also often sounded by Davis, would not be lost upon King. "When Schleiermacher," he wrote, "stressed the primacy of experience over any external authority, he was sounding a note that continues to live in my thought."[11]

Davis continued to use Clarke and Brown until the publication of L. Harold DeWolf's *A Theology of the Living Church* in 1953, an up-to-date volume essentially in the tradition of evangelical liberalism. The publication of this volume, during King's second year at Boston University, where DeWolf was King's major professor, was duly noted by King in a letter to Davis. King's remarks are very revealing because they show a close relationship between Davis, DeWolf, and King. King wrote:

> I have just finished reading your review of Dr. DeWolf's *A Theology of the Living Church* in the "Journal of Bible and Religion" and thought it was an excellent review. It was interesting to get

your reaction. It seems that my reaction was well nigh identical to yours. . . . Dr. DeWolf refers to himself as an evangelical liberal and, as I remember, this is about the position you hold. So you see that it was not difficult at all for me to emerge from your class- room to Dr. DeWolf's. I find the atmosphere in both classrooms saturated with a warm evangelical liberalism.[12]

Dr. Davis continued to use A Theology of the Living Church as the text in his required course in theology until his death in 1960. We are now in a position to inquire about Davis's interpreta- tion of evangelical liberalism and to elucidate his position more fully. Davis published an article in Theology Today just prior to King's enrollment at Crozer in 1948. At that time Theology Today was a relatively new journal published at Princeton Theologi- cal Seminary and had been established primarily to provide a forum for the dissemination of Barthianism and neoorthodoxy. Davis was asked to write an apologia for liberalism. In accor- dance with the approach of liberalism, Davis began the article, "In Praise of Liberalism," by arguing that liberalism is first and foremost a methodology (i.e., a spirit of inquiry), not a creedal statement. However, Davis was keenly aware that liberals, in fact, shared certain common beliefs. Thus, he went on to de- scribe those beliefs as the "positive message" of liberalism or what Harry Emerson Fosdick had called "abiding truths in changing categories." Although Davis identified eleven cardinal tenets of liberalism in the article,[13] they may be summarized as they ap- pear in Davis's writings as follows: (1) the existence of a moral order in the universe (cosmos); (2) the activity of God in his- tory; (3) the value of the personal; (4) the social character of human existence; (5) the ethical nature of Christian faith. We must now explain what Davis meant by these beliefs and how he developed them.

The first major theme of Davis's thought is the existence of a moral order in the universe. Davis's articles abound with both direct and indirect references to a moral law which infuses the world just as there are physical laws which support it. God has a purpose for the human race, and history moves toward a moral goal. Progress toward that goal may appear to be slow, but the outcome is certain, for there is a moral order "which is relevant to the corporate life of men and the ordering of human society. If mankind is to escape chaos and recurrent war, social and political institutions must be brought into conformity with this moral order."[14]

The ancient faith that "the stars in their courses fought against Sisera" is also true today. There is no theme in the thought of King more prominent than Davis's belief in the existence of a moral order. King's modern Sisera was the stubborn sheriff in Selma, Alabama, who "stumbled against the future" and helped to pass the Voting Rights Act of 1965 by handling Negroes in the Southern tradition.[15] (King's belief in the moral order will be discussed at some length in chapter 5.)

The second major theme of Davis's thought is that *God acts in history*, a theme integral to his affirmation of the existence of a moral order. Religious humankind, he argues, has always affirmed that there is a divine purpose in history, and the evidence proves that this is a rational belief. That God works within the processes of history is another way of saying that the universe is under spiritual control. In Davis's view, the belief in spiritual control sharply distinguishes the Judeo-Christian theological view of history from the Greek philosophical view of history. Biblical faith affirms that history, the events of which are given dynamic direction by God, is moving toward the triumph of righteousness as a goal rather than a mere repetition of endless cycles. Biblical faith sees God in the blood, sweat, and tears of human life, not in the meditation and solitude of the mystic. The biblical view of history sees God at work within earthly events. "Historic events do not just happen. They are done by God."[16]

Throughout King's writings and activities one finds a similar emphasis upon the importance of history and God's constant involvement in the historical process. "[God]," King affirmed with confidence, "is not outside the world looking on with a sort of cold indifference.... Like an ever-loving Father, he is working through history for the salvation of his children. As we struggle to defeat the forces of evil, the God of the universe struggles with us."[17] Hence, the Exodus event was a dominant theme in King's speeches and writings. That event, the model *par excellence* of God's involvement in history, was viewed by King as the most appropriate symbol for the civil rights movement. As God had delivered Israel from bondage to freedom, God would also deliver black people from slavery to liberation. King seems to have been able to convince his followers in the civil rights movement that God was active in history. For example, when the announcement that the Supreme Court had declared bus segregation unconstitutional came to Montgomery on November 13, 1956, a bystander exclaimed, "God Almighty has spoken from Washington, D.C."[18]

A third theme of Davis's thought is *the high priority assigned to the value of personality in Christian faith.* Without entering into an extensive discussion of personalism, a subject to be discussed later at some length, it is necessary to indicate here that the category of the personal was very significant for Davis, and that he had been influenced a great deal by the personalist philosophy of Borden Parker Bowne and Edgar S. Brightman. Davis regularly taught two courses on philosophy of religion, and King took both of them during his senior year. Whereas in many theological seminaries during the twenties, thirties, and forties, philosophy of religion had usurped the place of systematic theology, Davis continued to carry forward both disciplines at the same time, seeing no apparent conflict. Since God is the author of all truth, he used to say often, God is the source of the "rational" truths of philosophy of religion as well as the "revealed" truths of theology.

The principal textbooks Davis used in his courses on philosophy of religion indicate his approach: E. A. Burtt's *Types of Religious Philosophy,* D. C. Macintosh's *Theology as an Empirical Science,* and Edgar S. Brightman's *A Philosophy of Religion.* The personalism of Brightman, strongly influenced by philosophical idealism, was by far the single most important philosophical influence upon Davis. Whereas some scholars have argued that there was a fundamental difference between the theological liberalism of Clarke and Brown and the positions of Macintosh and

Brightman, this difference was more methodological than substantive. That is, in spite of a methodological difference with Clarke and Brown, both Macintosh and Brightman were essentially evangelical liberals in the content of their theology. At any rate, neither Davis nor King saw any conflict; they were advocates of both personalism and evangelical liberalism. The point is that King's introduction to personalism took place in Davis's courses where Brightman was the key figure.

How then did Davis interpret personalism? By "personal" Davis did not mean individualism or the differences which distinguish one person from another, but rather "that potential quality of life which separates *homo sapiens* from all other forms of creation and, indeed, lifts him above them."[19] In typical liberal fashion, Davis's affirmation of the value of the personal was grounded upon a prior belief concerning the nature of God's relationship to us. God is conceived as a loving Parent; we, God's children, are objects of God's compassion and concern. This is the reason that humankind must be conceived as "supremely worthful" and "inherently valuable."

Davis linked his belief in the value of the personal with Jesus of Nazareth and Jesus' emphasis upon the ethic of love. In Jesus of Nazareth we perceive the divine in the human and the intention of God for human life. God's love for humankind was revealed in the life and death of Jesus, and Jesus' sacrifice on the cross attested to the fact that every person is a being of infinite worth. The greatness of Christianity lies in its faith that the proper category for understanding the nature of ultimate reality is personality. Therefore, King defined personalism as " . . . the theory that the clue to the meaning of ultimate reality is found in personality. This personal idealism remains today my basic philosophical position."[20]

The fourth major theme in the thought of Davis is the conviction that *human existence is fundamentally social in character and that human solidarity is the goal toward which history evolves.* People are essentially social animals, and it is only within a context of fellowship and cooperation that an individual's character can evolve the way God intended it to evolve. Mature personality and character do not grow and develop among groups where individualism is the lifestyle. "It is much more likely to grow in democratic, cooperative, and Christian societies where people are constantly exhorted to manifest regard for the personal rights and opportunities of others."[21] The spirit of all mature religions is social, and sociality does not stifle individuality or suffocate the personal. To the contrary, it nurtures healthy interrelationships and interdependence. That is what we should expect because God's intention is that human life will become increasingly social and that humanity will achieve solidarity.

For Davis the goal of human history is increasing sociality. He offered as evidence for this assertion three major shifts he believed to be discernible in the development of history. The first shift has been from the external to the internal (i.e., from rite and custom to inner attitude); the second from the impersonal to the personal (i.e., from the treatment of people as things to the recognition of them as persons); the third from the individual to the social (i.e., from individualism to a love that is inclusive and which unites all humankind).[22] By the last shift Davis meant that a universal human community is the *terminus ad quem* history moves. He contends that Jesus never allowed his contemporary Jews to believe that Israel was the final loyalty. Since the purpose of God extends to all human life, no genuine community can be achieved by absolutizing a nation, tribe, or race. (Needless to say, this note struck a responsive nerve in King.) In this connection Davis refers approvingly to what Archbishop Temple had called the creation of the "Commonwealth of Value," characterized by "the slow realization of God's intention in history. Completed, it will usher in God's kingdom on earth."[23]

It seems apparent that when Davis claims, "We know now that we must live together or perish. If we will not have one world, we may have no world"[24] — he presages one of the main themes of King, the oft-quoted statement that the choice of humankind is not between violence and nonviolence but nonviolence and nonexistence.

The fifth theme of Davis is another classical tenet of liberalism: *Christianity is essentially a moral and ethical religion.* A familiar way to express Davis's point is that the goal and test of the Christian faith are its ethical fruits. Davis was concerned throughout his thought to balance the traditional supernatural interpretation of salvation with an ethical interpretation because he felt that the latter had been overshadowed by the former. He approached this subject by observing that Jesus "makes the goal of human character likeness in moral quality to God himself. . . ."[25] The way to become morally like God is to enter into complete fellowship with God and to do so is to experience what Jesus meant by "Sonship." When a person becomes like God in his or her ethical orientation (i.e., exhibits the qualities of love and forgiveness), he or she becomes a child of God. Jesus' words, Davis argues, are explicit: "Love your enemies . . . that ye may be sons." The Christian's ineradicable interest in the good life for all human beings stems from the ethical nature of the Christian faith and the moral foundation of Christian salvation. This theme is explicit in King's emphasis upon the Sermon on the Mount as the model for Christian behavior.

It is evident from this analysis of Davis's "positive message" of liberalism that he stood squarely within the camp of the evangelical liberals as described above. It is equally evident that evangelical liberalism is the term which most aptly describes King at this stage of his intellectual pilgrimage. Speaking of where he had arrived in his thinking at the close of his second year at Crozer, King said that he had become so convinced of the truth of the tenets of evangelical liberalism that he "almost fell into the trap of accepting uncritically everything it encompassed."[26]

Most of the major themes of Martin Luther King were the themes of evangelical liberalism. His stress upon the parenthood of God and the unity of humankind, the centrality of religious experience, the concern of God for all of life, the rights of humankind and moral feeling, the humanity of Jesus and his emphasis upon love, the dynamic nature of history and God's action therein, his essential optimism about human nature and history, the tolerance and openness of the liberal spirit, his tolerance toward a pluralism of world religions — all of these were key themes of evangelical liberalism embraced quite early in his intellectual pilgrimage. What we are contending, therefore, is that Davis, representing the distillation of liberal thought and the irenic spirit of the liberal mind, introduced King to the major motifs of King's mature thought. King would continue to develop, to broaden, and to criticize these themes, but he found them first in clearly articulated form in the evangelical liberalism of George Washington Davis.

To say that King should be viewed essentially as an evangelical liberal is not to infer that he did, in fact, fall "into the trap of accepting uncritically everything that it encompassed." King did develop second thoughts about some of the emphases of liberalism, and once again the influence of Davis seems to have been decisive. During the latter part of his career, Davis became increasingly critical of what he called "a liberalism without depth." This development in Davis's thought was undoubtedly a reaction to the negativism he found all too prevalent among many of his Crozer colleagues in whose minds liberalism simply meant the higher criticism of the Bible.

Davis set forth these reservations for the first time in print in one of his last articles in *The Crozer Quarterly*. It was published shortly after King's graduation from Crozer. In the article "Liberalism and a Theology of Depth," Davis was obviously somewhat defensive and apologetic about some of liberalism's failures and inadequacies. At the outset, he asserted that Christianity is first and foremost a religion of depth. He explained:

> By depth...Christianity breaks through the surface phenomena of existence, penetrating the mere events of history, the face of nature, and the physical life of man to bring an apprehension of what controls history, what glorifies the face of nature and what motivates man as a spiritual entity.[27]

In the explanation which follows, Davis distinguished between three levels of Christianity: the surface, the externals like ceremony, ritual, sacred books, etc.; the subsurface, the life of Jesus, the history of the church, and the uniqueness of denominational expression; and the depth which consists of the roots in human experience out of which all of the rest have come.

The point that Davis was trying to put across was that liberalism had often been so preoccupied with the surface and subsurface dimensions of Christianity that the depth dimension had been virtually ignored, in spite of the fact that this dimension had been responsible for the beginning of Christianity. Davis did not disavow, to be sure, the liberal's right to be critical; he was much too good a liberal himself to do that. Nevertheless, he seriously questioned what he called "a growing weakness" of liberalism which he located in its failure "to grasp the Bible as a whole, an apprehension which is impossible without an appreciation of the depths which it constantly plumbs."[28] By this he meant that an overemphasis upon such things as date and authorship of certain books, interpolations and inconsistencies in the text, historical context, and cultural factors had not only confused many sincere Christians but had also obscured the most important subject, the religious truths and meanings of Scripture.

In his call for a theology of depth Davis was attempting to maintain a balance between negative criticism and the message of the gospel of Jesus of Nazareth. He pleaded for the liberalism he knew and loved to disclose all facets of Christian faith and to go "beneath biblical criticism, historical perspective, and adjustment to contemporary thought and culture to ferret out those depths which made Christianity possible in the first place and which render it a live option today."[29] The indispensable element needed for a revitalized liberalism is a depth theology — one which takes into consideration all facets of Christian history, community, and experience.

Martin Luther King was aware of Davis's call for a theology of depth, and he would later incorporate Davis's insights in his own reassessment of liberalism. In a letter to Davis while still a student at Boston University, King, after acknowledging his debt to Davis and liberalism, goes on to say that he had come to see more merit in neoorthodoxy than he had previously because its emphasis upon transcendence (i.e., depth) seemed to be a necessary corrective to liberalism's almost exclusive emphasis upon immanence, which tended to lead it to accommodate too readily to modern culture. "At this point," King wrote appreciatively, "I have found your article, 'Liberalism and a Theology of Depth,' quite influential in my thinking. Neo-Orthodoxy certainly has the merit of calling us back to the depths of the Christian faith."[30]

In the course of his reflections on the inadequacies of liberalism, King goes so far as to comment favorably on the contribution of a well-known critic of liberalism: "Reinhold Niebuhr," he says, "probably more than any other thinker in America, has stressed the need of a 'dimension of depth' transcending nature, transcending history, if ethical action here and now is to be sustained by a faith that touches absolute bottom."[31] However, one should not infer from this accolade to Niebuhr that King ever abandoned evangelical liberalism, and the material which follows will clearly show this to be the case. It simply means that Niebuhr's critique of liberalism at certain points was presented with such persuasive logic that King could not ignore it. Since the Niebuhrian influence upon King will be treated in chapter 4, the point to be made here is that Davis's stress upon the transcendent (i.e., depth) dimension of Christianity undoubtedly prepared King to be more receptive to some of the insights of Niebuhr than he would have been otherwise. Be this as it may, King would attempt to combine some of the insights of Niebuhr with evangelical liberalism, and this attempt would pose tension points in King's mind that would remain unresolved at the time of his death.

CHAPTER TWO

Walter Rauschenbusch and the Social Gospel Movement

O NE OF THE MANIFESTATIONS of evangelical liberalism was the
social gospel movement. We are not surprised to find,
given the formative influence of evangelical liberalism upon King
through Davis, that King acknowledged a great debt to the social
gospel movement and to Walter Rauschenbusch. King confessed
that he found the theological basis for his social concern in the
thought of Rauschenbusch. He wrote:

> . . . Rauschenbusch gave to American Protestantism a sense of so-
> cial responsibility that it should never lose. The gospel at its best
> deals with the whole man, not only his soul but also his body,
> not only his spiritual well-being but also his material well-being.
> A religion that professes a concern for the souls of men and is
> not equally concerned about the slums that damn them, the eco-
> nomic conditions that strangle them, and the social conditions
> that cripple them, is a spiritually moribund religion.[1]

This meant to King that a religion that focuses exclusively upon
the individual is a truncated form of religion. To understand the
full import of this testimony to Rauschenbusch, we must outline
Rauschenbusch's thought and provide an overview of the social
gospel movement in general.

THE SOCIAL GOSPEL MOVEMENT

Since the social gospel movement had a long history and many
exponents, it is necessary to make some brief observations about

the movement in general in order to see Rauschenbusch in proper perspective. Contrary to the assumption of some people, liberalism and the social gospel were not synonymous. Liberalism was a many-sided movement, and the social gospel movement was only one of its manifestations. While nearly all of the exponents of the social gospel were liberals in theology, there were many who called themselves liberals who did not embrace the social gospel. (Dr. Morton Scott Enslin, noted earlier, is an excellent example.) The explanation for this fact is that whereas liberalism per se was primarily the result of the attempt to adjust traditional Christian thought to the impact of modern science and biblical criticism, the social gospel movement was also a response to another phenomenon, the new society which had emerged in the United States after the Civil War.

The social gospel movement in the United States, as it had been in Western Europe, was, in part, a response to the Industrial Revolution. But this should not be interpreted to mean, as some critics have alleged, that the social gospel was simply a response to external conditions and was without theological foundations or that the theology of the social gospel was an afterthought. The theology of the social gospel had been provided by evangelical liberalism. The teachings of Jesus as they had come to be interpreted by the exponents of the social gospel were joined with the rapid growth of sociological studies and interests. The social gospel movement, properly speaking, was the result of the convergence of new theological concepts and new sociological developments in the United States immediately following the Civil War.

The rapid industrialization and urbanization of society in the United States during the decades immediately following the Civil War produced a multitude of social and human problems. The tremendous industrial expansion between 1860 and 1890 increased the gross wealth of the United States from sixteen to sixty-five billion dollars. Since over 50 percent of the gross national product, however, had become concentrated in about forty thousand families or about one-third of 1 percent of the total population, the economic position of the industrial worker did not improve. Real wages during this period actually declined, as a consequence of which it became impossible for the worker to provide even the minimal necessities of life for himself and his family. He worked in unsanitary factories, lived in dark tenements, and spent most of his waking hours at backbreaking toil without a living wage. Thus, in the process of creating wealth such as the world had never seen, the Industrial Revolution also produced a disillusioned proletariat resentful of the poverty it had received as its share of the bounty.

The challenge with which the new society confronted American Protestantism was as urgent as the challenge presented by evolution and biblical criticism; besides, that challenge was both immediate and practical. Accepting the social status quo as the expression of the will of God, however, Protestantism, in the main, remained aloof from the new social challenge. Some of the most prominent church leaders were the most ardent defenders of laissez-faire capitalism (e.g., Henry Ward Beecher). After all, had not John Calvin proclaimed that wealth is a sign of divine favor and poverty is a judgment upon sin? As a result of its intransigence, American Protestantism came to the end of the nineteenth century ill-equipped to meet the needs of the new society. H. Richard Niebuhr aptly notes:

> The evangelical doctrine of the kingdom was not adequate for the new situation. . . . It could not emancipate itself from the conviction . . . that the human unit is the individual. It was unable therefore to deal with social crisis, with national disease and the misery of human groups.[2]

The character of the new society necessitated drastic modifications and readjustments in the Protestant ethic in order to be relevant to the new age. The social gospel movement should be understood, therefore, as an attempt to effect such changes in the traditional Protestant ethos. The major theological assumption that inspired the movement was that salvation had a social as well as an individual dimension and that social institutions had to be "saved" as well as individuals. For the exponents of the social gospel all economic problems had a moral dimension; the Christian ethic of love had to be considered as well as the laws of the market. This meant that in addition to charity, the church should also be concerned about social justice and with social structures as well as the individual morality of workers and business people. To this end, the advocates of the social gospel set out to ethicize and to socialize the classical doctrines of Christian theology. The most profound and enduring expression of that reinterpretation is found in the thought of Walter Rauschenbusch.

WALTER RAUSCHENBUSCH

If a poll were taken among Christians familiar with the history of Protestantism on the question, "Who have been our twentieth-century prophets?" the name of Walter Rauschenbusch would certainly be near the top of the list. Walter Rauschenbusch (1861–1918) was reared in the individualistic, conservative pietism of a German Lutheran family turned Baptist. He was born in Rochester, New York, and he spent all of his life there except for eleven years as a pastor in New York City. With the exception of two short periods of study in Germany, where he was introduced to the thought of Ritschl and Harnack, he received his education in his hometown, graduating from the University of Rochester in 1884 and from Rochester Theological Seminary in 1886. After his graduation from seminary, he went to be pastor of the Second German Baptist Church in New York City on the edge of the depressed Hell's Kitchen area (W. 145th Street, Manhattan). He returned to Rochester in 1897 to teach first in the field of New Testament and later Church History at his alma mater, Rochester Theological Seminary. He became a nationally known figure with the publication of *Christianity and the Social Crisis* in 1907, and he remained in Rochester until his death in 1918.[3]

During his pastorate in Hell's Kitchen, working among people

who were out of work and out of hope, the young pastor began to question the theology he had learned in seminary. In the
crucible of the experience of Hell's Kitchen, Rauschenbusch began to raise questions about the adequacy of the individualistic
approach of Protestant orthodoxy as he came to appreciate the
influence of social conditions upon human personality and character. For these reasons, he began to study the Bible and the
Christian tradition again to find out what they had to say about
social evil. As a result of an intensive study of the Prophets,
Jesus, and the early church, later to be included as the first
three chapters of *Christianity and the Social Crisis,* he professed to
find a profound concern for the social dimension of life running
throughout. In his view, traditional interpretations of Christianity had failed to comprehend that sin and salvation were social
facts, not just theological doctrines.

In spite of his concern about the social dimensions of Christianity, Rauschenbusch did not dichotomize the individual and
the social or the religious and the ethical. He observed that
while the Bible stressed the primacy of the religious dimension
(i.e., the individual's relationship with God), it also located the
test and goal of religion in social concern and social justice respectively. Robert Handy suggests that Rauschenbusch found the
basis for his version of the social gospel in the Bible and especially in "the doctrine of the kingdom of God, which brought
together his evangelical concern for individuals and his social vision of a redeemed society."[4] Rauschenbusch's literary works were
an *apologia* for the necessary relationship between the Christian church and social issues. His overriding concern was, "How
does the biblical message relate to social structures of human
community?"

Today is not the best time to attempt to summarize the
thought of Walter Rauschenbusch because the research is in a
state of flux. In recent years many scholars have begun seriously to question many of the generally accepted neoorthodox
stereotypes of Rauschenbusch's theology and ethics.[5] It is safe to
say that no fully adequate account of Rauschenbusch's thought

will be possible until this research has been completed. For the purpose of this study, fortunately, we do not have to await the outcome of the research or to resolve the issues involved in the debate, because those aspects of Rauschenbusch's thought that influenced King, either rightly or wrongly conceived, are quite clear. It is also fortunate that while most of Rauschenbusch's major themes are evident in King's thought, there were certain key concepts more directly important than others. These key concepts are: (1) the prophetic model of religion, (2) the relationship between the church and the world, and (3) the kingdom of God and human community.

The Prophetic Model: Religion as Ethical and Social

The chapter, "The Historical Roots of Christianity," on the Hebrew prophets in *Christianity and the Social Crisis* is one of the most perceptive in all the literature on the subject. All of the major themes of Rauschenbusch's version of the social gospel are found in fetal form in this analysis of the nature and function of the biblical prophet. Since this was one of the few books ever referred to specifically by King, it must have had a profound impact. One can imagine the excitement with which King, a twenty-year-old, alert seminary student searching for a theological basis for his social concern, must have read this evangelical and zealous account of Rauschenbusch's heroes of religion. At any rate, King's own appreciation of the prophets would become equally as evangelical and enthusiastic.

Rauschenbusch argued that Jesus stood squarely in the tradition of the Old Testament prophets and that Christianity was the direct heir of the priority assigned to the social dimension of life by the prophets of Israel. Moreover, whenever Christianity has attempted to change social and political conditions for the betterment of humankind, it has manifested its indebtedness to the social ideals of the Old Testament because they have made, when properly understood and interpreted, positive contributions to the development of democracy and social justice in Western culture. In the thought of the prophets, the poor and the godly were often identified; the Old Testament speaks of the wicked rich man and the blessed poor man. This theme was repeated in the Magnificat, wherein the lowly are exalted and the mighty are humbled. Christianity became the heir of the prophetic tradition primarily through the Jewish-Christian communities that comprised the radical social wing of the early church. The classic expressions of the prophetic spirit in the New Testament are the synoptic gospels and the Epistle of James — Rauschenbusch called the latter "one of the most democratic books of the New Testament."[6]

The essence of the prophetic principle, according to Rauschenbusch, is *the affirmation of historical relativity* — everything in history stands under the judgment of God. For this reason, the prophet cannot put a stamp of approval upon anything "as it is." The prophet must always point out the gap between the will of God and "the present order of things." No person who calls himself or herself a Christian can accept "things as they are"; instead, one must condemn them on the basis of the values enunciated by the prophets and Jesus.

Rauschenbusch goes on to explain that the prophetic model also includes religious fervor, a democratic spirit, a strong social conscience, and free utterance of one's belief. The combination of such factors produced the Hebrew prophets and all of the radical movements in Christianity. All of those movements have posited a radical tension between "what ought to be" (i.e., God's will) and "what is" (i.e., the present order). Hence, Rauschenbusch warns modern Christians who wish to be prophetic that they will have to risk the charge of partisanship; the wider the social cleavages, the more difficult it will be to satisfy both sides. Nevertheless, the modern prophet should not be deterred by such pitfalls and should forge ahead anyway because it is not

his business to try trimming and straddling. He must seek to hew as straight as the moral law. Let others voice special interest; the minister of Jesus Christ must voice the mind of Jesus Christ. His strength will lie in the high impartiality of moral insight and love to all.[7]

One of the corollaries of the prophetic model of religion in Rauschenbusch's thought is *the inseparability of religion and ethics.* If one believes in the social gospel, any method of cultivating the spiritual life may be chosen provided it has an ethical outcome. Righteousness is what God demands; an ethical life is the appropriate act of worship; and the amelioration of social injustice is the goal of the religious person. During its early history, Christianity embodied the prophetic conviction that the service of God is ethical conduct (i.e., right relations with one's fellow humans), not ritual and ceremony. If Christianity had retained that original thrust, "it would have been an almost inconceivable leap forward in social and religious evolution."[8] We must see Rauschenbusch's suspicion of mysticism in this context. His suspicion was based on his observation of the facility with which people often avoid responsibility to their neighbors by taking refuge in God. Rauschenbusch was adamant that an adequate relationship to God is impossible if it does not include the dimension of social responsibility.

Another corollary of the prophetic model of religion, for Rauschenbusch, is *the affirmation of the fundamental social character of religion.* To be more exact, he claimed that this should be the major norm for judging religion. In support of this view, he observed that the community of Israel produced the prophets. They were not isolated, autonomous individuals but an integral part of a covenantal community. They were not produced by a religion focused exclusively upon the individual; a religion so oriented may breed "saints, missionaries, pastors, and scholars, but few prophets."[9] There must be a "community-oriented" religion for the prophetic gift to emerge. The record shows, he contends, that people of the modern age who have had a sense of prophetic vision and power of language to express it have had a "social enthusiasm and faith in the reconstructive power of Christianity."[10]

Rauschenbusch's exposition of the prophetic model of religion emphasized the point that the prophets stressed public instead of private morality. Since their eyes were focused on public morality, the evils condemned by them in the name of Yahweh were injustice and oppression. The basic sympathies of Jesus were also with the poor and the outcasts. Rauschenbusch's passion and power of argument reaches unparalleled heights in his support of those sympathies of the prophets and Jesus, and his persuasive rhetoric certainly was duly noted by King. Rauschenbusch's own life and writings, manifesting a deep concern for the poor and a pervasive egalitarian strain, were also a source of great inspiration for King. He agreed with Rauschenbusch that if the prophets and Jesus had limited their vision to an individualism like that of modern Christianity, their unique contribution to religion, ethical monotheism, would never have been formulated.

The Hebrew prophets influenced King more than any other part of Scripture with the exception of the Sermon on the Mount. Sometimes by direct quotation, but mostly by tone and implication, the prophetic model is evident in most of King's speeches and writings. He called frequently for a revolution in values based on the Beatitudes and Isaiah 40:4 (KJV): "Every valley shall be exalted, and every mountain and hill shall be made low: and the crooked shall be made straight, and the rough places plain. . . ." He used over and over again the famous passage from Amos 5:24: "But let judgment run down as waters, and righteousness as a mighty stream." The revolution he envisaged would be waged in the cause of justice for all people, but especially the black citizens of the United States. When he was tried in court before Judge Loe in September, 1958, he told the judge that it would be contrary to his conscience to pay the fine, but he would readily accept the alternative of the court without malice. His reasoning typifies the prophetic tradition: "My action is motivated by the impelling voice of conscience and a desire to follow the truth and the will of God wherever they lead. . . ."[11]

Martin Luther King had the prophetic insight to discern the difference between a false and a true peace, and by way of

explanation he pointed out that the Montgomery boycott simply revealed that the surface of order and tranquillity was a false
peace. When he was criticized for the disruption between the
races caused by the boycott, he speculated that that must have
been what Jesus meant when he said: "I have not come to bring
peace but a sword," a figurative way of lashing out against false
peace. King saw his mission in a similar way: "Whenever I come,
a division sets in between justice and injustice. I have come to
bring a positive peace which is the presence of justice, love.... "[12]
King was greatly disheartened that the church had often supported a false peace. He did not think that one had to look
very hard to discover that the church had not always followed
the will of God but rather had sanctioned immoral and uneth-
ical practices, such as slavery, war, segregation, and economic
exploitation.

The Relationship between Church and Society

Rauschenbusch's views on the relationship between church and
society also had a significant influence upon the thought of Martin Luther King. Rauschenbusch's most caustic remarks on this
subject were directed against the position, alleged by him to have
been the dominant position for over fifteen hundred years, that
the world (i.e., society "as it is") is essentially evil and that withdrawal from it is the only way to practice the authentic Christian
life. He was quick to point out, anticipating those who would
claim that the church had had a significant impact upon society,
that the social effects often attributed to the church had never
actually constituted a reordering of society according to Christian values. He was firmly convinced that the so-called reforms,
in fact, had been a defense of the social evils of the time.

Believing the strategy of withdrawal to be out of the question
for the modern Christian, he concluded that there are only two
alternatives: "The Church must either condemn the world and
seek to change it, or tolerate the world and conform to it."[13]
Rauschenbusch, of course, advocated the former alternative, and

he urged the church to follow the teachings of Jesus and to be-come an agent of change. He saw a major conflict between the teachings of Jesus and the major institutions of capitalism in the United States. He believed that the church would be more effec-tive in combating the evils of society if it abandoned the indirect approach through individuals and made a direct assault upon unjust institutions.

Rauschenbusch manifested a healthy respect for the power of social structures, or what he called "the super-personal forces in the community."[14] He proceeded to explain that just as repen-tance is required of an individual, so there must be repentance for social sins because evil has a structural character. When fun-damentalists, therefore, remind the advocates of a better social order that they do not know enough about the depth of sin in the human heart, the fundamentalists should be reminded that they are far too unrealistic about the intransigence of sinful so-cial structures and that they often bow before "one of the devil's spider-webs, praising it as one of the mighty works of God."[15] Rauschenbusch's point is that regeneration means that Christians should be subject to the law of Christ in both their personal and social relationships. The final test of religion is whether individual piety produces social fruits.

All of the emphases of Rauschenbusch's views on the relation-ship between church and society are echoed in the thought of King. In no uncertain terms, King called the church to respon-sibility for and involvement in the social order. "It has always been," he proclaimed without hesitation, "the responsibility of the church to broaden horizons, challenge the status quo, and break the mores when necessary."[16] To turn this point around, King disagreed emphatically with those who held that the church should not become involved in social issues. Since the church is the ethical and religious authority in the community, it must con-stantly address itself to social problems and use its power in the struggle for social justice.

The social problem that dominated King's concern, at least until late in his career, was racism. Throughout his writings, the church is taken to task for its failures in this area. It was beyond his comprehension how anyone observing the history of the church in the United States could deny "the shameful fact that it [church] has been an accomplice in structuring racism into the architecture of American society."[17] By sanctioning slavery and embracing segregation, the church had failed to fulfill its historic mission. Hence, some of King's severest language is reserved for the "faithless church." Since the church is the most segregated major institution in American society, it has become "an echo rather than a voice, a taillight behind the Supreme Court and other secular agencies, rather than a headlight guiding men progressively and decisively to higher levels of understanding."[18]

King firmly believed that the church should take the lead in programs of social action and social change. By this he meant that the church should combat injustices black people confront in the areas of housing, education, employment, legal problems, etc. If it were to take an active role in these areas, people would once again see the church as the bulwark of justice and peace. Wherever the church has so witnessed, it has been a powerful influence for the common good of the community. In this connection King recalled that the early Christians suffered gladly for their faith, not content to be thermometers "that recorded the ideas and principles of popular opinion," but thermostats "that transformed the mores of society."[19] For King it was absolutely essential for the church to recapture its prophetic zeal and to participate actively in the struggle for economic and racial justice and peace between the nations of the world. That would be the only way for the church to demonstrate to the world that it is a community of love.

King, himself, practiced what he preached about the church's relationship to society. Since he was somewhat embarrassed by the "silk stocking" image of his first parish, Dexter Avenue Baptist Church in Montgomery, Alabama, he was anxious at the very beginning of his ministry there to open the church to all classes and to provide a common meeting ground for people of every segment of society. One of the first innovations of the young, alert, and sensitive pastor was to set up a Social and Political Action Committee as an expression of his concern for voter registration. He became involved personally in several local committees, including the local branch of the National Association for the Advancement of Colored People and the Alabama Council of Human Relations.

Behind King's firm belief that the church has a responsibility for the social needs of the world was one of his central theological assumptions, the unity of the body and the soul. He went to great lengths to show that Christianity has a double focus. "On the one side, it seeks to change the souls of men and thereby unite them with God; on the other, it seeks to change the environmental conditions of men so that the soul will have a chance after it is changed."[20] Although King did not distinguish between Hebraic religion and Hellenic philosophy as Rauschenbusch had, he contrasted "biblical" religion and "other-worldly" religion and noted that the latter makes "a strange, un-Biblical distinction between body and soul, between the sacred and the secular."[21] Whereas other-worldly religion considers life to be essentially evil, biblical religion sees it "whole" and pronounces it "good."

In one of the early mass meetings held in connection with the Montgomery bus boycott, Dr. Frazier, a Methodist minister, scandalized by the fact that the leaders of the boycott were ministers, expressed the position King was trying to combat when he exclaimed: "The job of the minister is to lead the souls of men to God, not to bring about confusion by getting tangled up in transitory social problems."[22] King's response is a succinct statement of his theological rationale for the involvement of the church in social issues. "I can see no conflict," he retorted, "between our devotion to Jesus Christ and our present action. In fact I see a necessary relationship. If one is truly devoted to the religion of Jesus he will seek to rid the earth of social evils. The gospel is social as well as personal."[23] King was just as adamant as Rauschenbusch that social conditions "be saved," or as we would say "humanized."

The Kingdom of God and Human Community

An understanding of Rauschenbusch's interpretation of the kingdom of God and its relationship to the ideal of an inclusive human community is absolutely essential in order to comprehend King's conception of "The Beloved Community." The concept of the kingdom of God was Rauschenbusch's central, all-pervading theme. It was the pivotal doctrine of his major theological work, *A Theology for the Social Gospel,* wherein he insists that theology "must not only make room for the doctrine of the Kingdom of God, but give it a central place and revise all other doctrines so that they will articulate organically with it."[24] The centrality of the doctrine of the kingdom of God led him to conclude that the Christian religion is essentially corporate and communal in character.

The one ever-present theme in Rauschenbusch's writings is that the kingdom of God is synonymous with a transformed and regenerated society. The primary purpose of Christianity is "to transform human society into the kingdom of God by regenerating all human relations and reconstituting them in accordance with the will of God."[25] The kingdom of God for Jesus denoted a complete restructuring of human society. The early church, heir of the tradition of Jesus and the prophets, looked forward to a new era when social life would be reorganized on a moral basis. More importantly, Rauschenbusch hastened to add, "The kingdom of God is still a collective conception, involving the whole social life of man. It is not a matter of saving human atoms, but of saving the social organism."[26] In short, the kingdom of God should be viewed as a social and collective hope within history.

On the basis of such assumptions, Rauschenbusch formulated his famous definitions of the kingdom of God: It is "humanity organized according to the will of God" and "the organized fellowship of humanity acting under the impulse of love."[27] Rauschenbusch often used "kingdom of God," "true human community," and "righteous community" interchangeably because each points to a society characterized by freedom, justice, equality, and love. It is clear that "humanity organized according to the will of God" and "humanity acting under the impulse of love" was a parallelism for Rauschenbusch. The parallelism embodies what Christ revealed — that human personality has permanent worth. "Since love is the supreme law of Christ," the kingdom means "a progressive reign of love in human affairs."[28] Love is best expressed as service to others; it might necessitate the surrender of one's property and privileges.

Having defined the kingdom of God in such terms, Rauschenbusch consistently went on to describe it in terms of an inclusive human community. The transformed society will be an open society, and it will transcend all divisions of nationality, race, and religion. Therefore, Rauschenbusch saw a real need to restore to Christianity the idea of the millennial hope which he thought had largely been omitted from the mainstream of Christianity. He did not wish to engage in setting time and place, but he did wish to justify the substance of the millennial hope, a future society characterized by love, justice, and peace.

Rauschenbusch attempted to avoid the charge of utopianism, and he did so by speaking of the kingdom as both present and future. Just as an individual Christian is "already" but "not yet," so the kingdom is always in the making. When the spirit of Christ has changed all the natural relations of humankind and given them a divine significance and value, the kingdom of God will have arrived. There is a definite realism about the historical possibilities of the kingdom in this statement:

> In asking for faith in the possibility of a new social order, we ask for no Utopian delusion. We know well that there is no perfection for man in this life: there is only growth toward perfection. . . . We make it a duty to seek what is unattainable. We have the same paradox in the perfectibility of society. We shall never have a perfect social life, yet we must seek it with faith.[29]

In spite of such qualifications, many of Rauschenbusch's critics still feel that he was too optimistic about the historical possibilities of the kingdom. Martin Luther King was cognizant of these critics, and he seems to have agreed with them up to a point. At any rate, he said on one occasion that Rauschenbusch seemed to have "fallen victim to the nineteenth-century 'cult of inevitable progress' which led him to a superficial optimism concerning man's nature."[30] The charge of superficial optimism has been generally accepted by many of Rauschenbusch's critics, but recent research seems to indicate that this is a caricature of his position. Whether King was right or wrong in his assessment of Rauschenbusch at this point, the fact remains that King was clearly indebted to him for his dream for the future, a key theme in King's thought. The understanding of the kingdom of God as inclusive human community was obviously the theological basis of King's "I-Have-a-Dream" theme. The full meaning of this aspect of King's thought will be treated in chapter 6, "The Vision of the Beloved Community."

CHAPTER THREE

Gandhi: Nonviolence and Civil Disobedience

THERE HAS BEEN a great deal of speculation about how King became acquainted with Gandhi and when he actually embraced nonviolence as a way of life. While the latter remains somewhat obscure even now and will probably never be resolved for certain, the facts about the former are more or less clear. An important event related to King's introduction to Gandhi was an address delivered by Mordecai Johnson at Fellowship House in Philadelphia in the spring of 1950. King had already heard the absolute pacifist line expounded at Crozer Seminary by A. J. Muste, but he had not been convinced of its validity.[1] However, Johnson's presentation of the thought of Gandhi was a different story. Perhaps it was the Howard University president's charisma and his deeply held convictions, or King's own receptivity at the time, or, more likely, a combination of all three; at any rate, King was motivated to purchase several books about Gandhi and to read them intensively.

While this story about Johnson is accurate, it is by no means the whole story about King's introduction to Gandhi. During the first term of King's senior year at Crozer after Johnson's speech, King took an elective course with George W. Davis on the psychology of religion, which included case studies of eminent religious personalities, such as Gandhi.[2] The only evidence, prior to this study of Gandhi with Davis, that King had studied any of the literature on pacifism, nonviolence, and civil disobedience is that he had read Thoreau's *Essay on the Duty of Civil Disobedience* in a philosophy class at Morehouse College. The essay stirred him greatly, and he reread it several times. Nevertheless, this initial encounter with Thoreau did not bear any immediate fruits.

The course with Davis was part lecture and part seminar; for the latter each student was required to research a major figure for an oral presentation before the class. King wrote his paper on Gandhi, perhaps because of the impact of Johnson's speech the previous spring. One of the authors of this book read the paper King wrote on Gandhi, but he does not remember anything about its contents, except the bibliography, which included those volumes and articles from the Bucknell Library at Crozer that he himself had used for a paper on Gandhi for the same course in the fall of 1947. The books were three volumes by Charles F. Andrews, *Mahatma Gandhi's Ideas, Mahatma Gandhi, Mahatma Gandhi at Work: His Own Story*; Romain Rolland, *Mahatma Gandhi: The Man Who Became One with Universal Being*; Mahatma Gandhi, *Autobiography: The Story of My Experiments with Truth*; and Richard B. Gregg's *The Power of Nonviolence*.

King's favorite book on the life and work of Gandhi was F. B. Fisher's *That Strange Little Brown Man, Gandhi* (1932). This is evident from King's obvious paraphrases of the title, "a little brown man in India"[3] and "the little brown saint of India."[4] These books, along with a collection of articles from *Friend's Intelligencer, Christian Advocate, Friend,* and *Student World,* had been placed in the Bucknell Library by Davis, who, as a pacifist and an admirer of Gandhi, had been interested in nonviolence as a means of social change for many years.

The point is that Mahatma Gandhi was no stranger at Crozer, and King was not the first liberal-minded student who had been attracted to the Gandhian philosophy of nonviolence. Across the years, in fact, many Crozer graduates had become members of The Fellowship of Reconciliation and The Baptist Pacifist Fellowship. That King was affected more profoundly than others goes without saying. He readily admitted that Gandhi's concept of *satyagraha* was "profoundly significant" for him, and that Gandhi persuaded him that love need not be sentimental, nor for weaklings, nor simply applicable to individual relationships, but that whole communities and nations could practice the "turn-the-other-cheek" philosophy of the Sermon on the Mount.

King's tribute to Gandhi, a statement revealing serious ethical probing and an interpretation of certain aspects of his own conception of Christian ethics, reads as follows:

> Gandhi was probably the first person in history to lift the love ethic of Jesus above mere interaction between individuals to a powerful and effective social force on a large scale. Love for Gandhi was a potent instrument for social and collective transformation. It was in this Gandhian emphasis on love and nonviolence that I discovered the method for social reform that I had been seeking for so many months.... I came to feel that this was the only morally and practically sound method open to oppressed people in their struggle for freedom.[5]

The key word in this quotation is "method" because King's "satisfaction" was with Gandhi's strategy and tactics. King's presuppositions for his interpretation of nonviolent resistance were derived from Christian theology and ethics, especially Jesus' teachings in the Sermon on the Mount and the concept of *agape*. By Gandhi's method, of course, King meant nonviolent resistance. King explained: "...Christ furnished the spirit and motivation, while Gandhi furnished the method."[6] Gandhi's method, too, presupposed certain philosophical and religious concepts, and it is necessary to understand them in order to understand his method.

GANDHI'S ASSUMPTIONS: *SATYAGRAHA* AND *AHIMSA*

It is generally agreed by experts on Gandhi that his system of thought was based upon two major philosophical or religious concepts, *satyagraha* and *ahimsa*. Space does not allow us to work our way through the thorny problems surrounding the sources of Gandhi's thought. Suffice it to say, he was undoubtedly supported and encouraged by John Ruskin, Leo Tolstoy,

Henry David Thoreau, Jesus, and the Sermon on the Mount. However, he probably was not *decisively* influenced by any non-Indian sources. His thought was essentially Indian, and all of his basic ideas can be found in the Indian religious tradition. "The more we study Mahatma Gandhi's own life and teaching," Charles F. Andrews observes, "the more certain it becomes that Hindu Religion has been the greatest of all influences in shaping his ideas and actions."[7] *Satyagraha* is a meaning-laden Sanskrit word, meaning "firmness in the truth," "holding fast to truth," or simply *truth-force*. It has come generally to mean the effort to improve social conditions through the use of *truth-force* (i.e., nonviolent resistance) instead of physical force (i.e., violence). Gandhi went to great lengths to distinguish *truth-force* from "passive resistance," the phrase often used to describe his position. *Truth-force* was viewed by Gandhi as a form of action, not passivity, a dynamic means of resistance that requires a great deal of courage and strength to practice effectively.

For Gandhi, *satya* (*truth*) is the spiritual or metaphysical basis of nonviolent resistance. There is a profound ontology associated with the etymology of the word. *Satya* is derived from *sat*, meaning "Being." Thus it seems that *sat* is a synonym for the reality called God in English. It has not been uncommon in Christian theology to use truth as an attribute of God, but Gandhi wished to go further and to affirm that truth is synonymous with God. Gandhi is saying, philosophically speaking, that *satya* is the most inclusive and comprehensive term available to talk about ultimate reality. Since *truth* is identified with ultimate reality in Gandhi's thinking, *truth* is also a synonym for soul or spirit. Hence, *satyagraha* is often referred to simply as *soul-force*.

Beginning with this ontological assumption, Gandhi went on to join ontology with ethics. The only objective criterion available to humanity to test *truth* is the human one (i.e., the fulfillment of human wants and needs). For example, *truth* in the famous March to the Sea in 1930 meant the basic right of Indians to have free access to their salt and to manufacture it as they saw fit. The *truth* which was the basis of the *Vykom satyagraha* was the right of every human being to walk the public road through the village and by the temple without regard to caste. Behind these and other campaigns of Gandhi was the fundamental belief in the right of a people to self-government. Such an inalienable right points to the ultimate source of *truth*. Secure in this belief, the *satyagrahi*, one who practices *satyagraha*, can confidently persevere because he or she knows that he or she is on the side of the moral law of the cosmos.

Gandhi often referred to God as having spoken to him, called him, guided him. His devotional life of prayer and meditation and his intellectual articulation of *satyagraha* both demonstrate the importance of God for him. In fact, he believed that the true *satyagrahi* has no power of his or her own; all power is derived from God. If the *satyagrahi* is faithful, God will provide assistance. The practical value of such a belief is related to the inordinate suffering the *satyagrahi* will undoubtedly have to undergo. Gandhi was well aware that most human beings are not adequately equipped to endure a great deal of humiliation and pain. In order to be strong and courageous, therefore, the *satyagrahi* needs the strength derived from God's assistance. God was Gandhi's "voice within" and the source of his moral authority. If asked how he could be certain he had discovered *truth* when listening to the "voice within," Gandhi would reply that one's readiness to suffer would tell. Prayer, fasting, and other acts of self-purification not only equipped Gandhi to be a *satyagrahi* but also enabled him to be a powerful agent of social change. *Satyagraha* became for Gandhi a total way of life — a way of dealing with all conflicts, interpersonal and social.

Closely related to *satyagraha*, but not identical with it, is Gandhi's other major concept, *ahimsa*. While many of Gandhi's critics have accused him of both ambiguity and inconsistency in his presentation of the meaning of *satyagraha*, there is general agreement about the exact meaning of *ahimsa*.[8] Erik H. Erikson postulates that *ahimsa* as used by Gandhi means two things: the refusal (1) to do harm to the opponent and (2) "to violate another person's essence."[9] In other words, the *satyagrahi* should always respect the *truth* of the opponent. If *truth* is relative, and it always is in the sense that no one can ever know all the *truth*, the coercion used against the opponent must not be for the purpose of punishment or retaliation.

In emphasizing this point, Erikson seems to have put his finger on the key to the power of *satyagraha*. While it sometimes confounded his followers, Gandhi's determination to follow this principle led him on numerous occasions to call off or suspend apparently successful campaigns because he perceived that other forces had changed his opponent's position, making him unfairly vulnerable. (King also would be accused of withdrawing several times apparently for the same reason.) However, such actions not only breathed power into Gandhi's movement, they also weakened the resolve of the opponent because of the newly perceived "fairness" of Gandhi and his followers. When viewed in this perspective, *ahimsa* thus becomes a trust-engendering principle. It was Gandhi's way of applying the spiritual (*truth*) to the sphere of action (*ahimsa*), hoping to avoid the pitfall of the self-righteous judgment of others.

The literal meaning of *ahimsa* is "non-injury" or "non-killing." The etymology of the word gives it a negative ring — the *a* meaning "no" and *himsa* meaning "injury." But Gandhi did not interpret *ahimsa* literally. Non-injury to any living thing, to be sure, is an element of *ahimsa* but it is the "least expression" of it, because *ahimsa* "is not merely a negative state of harmlessness but it is a positive state of love, of doing good even to the evil-doer."[10] In other words, Gandhi seems to have drawn an analogy between *ahimsa* and the Christian conception of *agape*. "Complete Nonviolence," Gandhi explained, "is complete absence of ill will against all that lives. . . . It is pure Love."[11] "The force of love," he added, "is the same as the force of soul or truth."[12] (King sometimes referred to *satyagraha* as *love-force*.) Most of Gandhi's interpreters agree that Gandhi added a new quality to Hindu ethics by linking *ahimsa* and love. "The especial contribution of Gandhi," Bondurant observes, "was to make the concept of *ahimsa* meaningful in the social and political spheres by moulding tools of nonviolent action to use as a positive force in the search for social and political truths."[13] It will become clear as we proceed that this was exactly the way Martin Luther King understood Gandhi.

GANDHI'S TACTICS: NONCOOPERATION AND CIVIL DISOBEDIENCE

Gandhi's strategy of nonviolent resistance, grounded upon the assumptions of *satyagraha* and *ahimsa*, was manifested primarily in two principal tactics, "noncooperation" and "civil disobedience." In Gandhi's thought, noncooperation included a broad range of responses to the evil aspects of the social system. It is conceived as less aggressive than the tactic of civil disobedience, though both were to be executed according to the spirit of *ahimsa*. To be more exact, noncooperation meant the withdrawal of cooperation at those points where the state had clearly become immoral and unjust. Noncooperation might take the form of rejection of certain services, such as schools, courts, or government bodies.

Noncooperation might also take the form of the operation of parallel institutions, such as the revival of village industries to produce cloth instead of purchasing it from the British. The spinning wheel thus became a symbol of noncooperation and the production of cloth by Indian villagers a form of social protest. The word most commonly used to denote such activity, of course, is *boycott*. Although Gandhi often raised questions about the moral validity of boycotts on the grounds that they might be construed as retaliatory and punitive, he thought the boycott of British cloth was clearly warranted. He was careful to make it quite clear, however, that the reason for the boycott of cloth was not because it was British but because the importation of cloth into India had made paupers of millions of people.

Gandhi's justification for noncooperation was predicated upon the assumption that all citizens have an inherent right not to cooperate with a government that refuses to pay any heed to their grievances. Although he held that citizens had the right to refuse to cooperate with an unjust government, he also insisted that a government seeking to eliminate evil should receive the citizen's support. (Needless to say, this distinction was very important for his interpretation of civil disobedience.) When asked repeatedly whether noncooperation was an end or a means to an end, he always replied that it would be the means whereby an unjust government would recover its true end, justice for all. When it was charged that noncooperation was essentially negative and passive, Gandhi responded that it was just the opposite: it is a positive and active state, because, deriving its force from *ahimsa,* it involves one totally, mind and body, attitude and action. In other words, rejection is as much a form of action as acceptance. This is the context in which Gandhi's famous statement, later to be echoed by King, should be understood: "Non-co-operation with evil is as much a duty as co-operation with good."[14]

Gandhi's other major tactic of nonviolent resistance was "civil disobedience." Civil disobedience, in his view, is one expression of *satyagraha,* but it is not synonymous with *satyagraha.* Gandhi's definition of civil disobedience reflects the classical understanding of it by social philosophers in general: *It is a civil breach of a law considered to be immoral.* That is to say, civil disobedience assumes that while one does not have a *legal* right to disobey a law considered to be unjust, one has a *moral* duty to do so. It follows that one must be willing to submit to the penalty for civil disobedience. For Gandhi this meant the cheerful acceptance of imprisonment and other hardships. Unlike a criminal lawbreaker who performs his acts under cover and seeks to avoid punishment, the nonviolent resister will suffer the penalty for disobedience without complaint.

As the last statement indicates, the jail became a very important symbol for Gandhi, and he urged his followers to seek arrest and imprisonment, just as a soldier is willing to die in battle. One manifestation of the success of nonviolent resistance is the presence of thousands of victims of oppression behind bars. "A-jail-is-a-jail-is-a-jail" for a criminal, but for Gandhi a jail was a palace.[15] (One recalls Thoreau's famous statement: "Under a government which imprisons any unjustly, the true place for a just man is also a prison."[16]) The possibility of imprisonment is the reason Gandhi held that civil disobedience requires a much higher degree of commitment and self-discipline than noncooperation.

Gandhi went to great lengths to distinguish between civil disobedience and anarchism. As he saw it, only criminal disobedience results in anarchy, and that is why every society rightly suppresses it. Gandhi always employed civil disobedience with great reluctance and called for it only as a last resort. Only the rarest cases led him to consider a law so unjust as to warrant the open violation of it. He called for civil disobedience only when it was clearly the only alternative to either resignation or physical force. The practitioner of civil disobedience must be one who freely, and as a matter of duty, usually obeys all laws of society. In other words, it means "the reluctant nonviolent disobedience of such laws as are in themselves bad and obedience to which would be inconsistent with one's self-respect or human dignity."[17]

Gandhi was constantly called upon to defend noncooperation and civil disobedience against the charge that they were subtle forms of violence or that they precipitated violence. (Reinhold Niebuhr, for example, argued against Gandhi that there is, in the final analysis, no intrinsic difference between violent and nonviolent resistance — an argument that would cause King a great deal of anguish.[18]) Gandhi freely admitted that noncooperation and civil disobedience involved the risk of violence, but he was quick to add that nonviolent resistance did not cause violence but simply allowed concealed hostilities to rise to the surface. Violence might emerge as a result of the use of civil disobedience, but civil disobedience will not be the cause of violence. The reason(s) for violence will be present, already eating away silently at the fabric of social relations. Although Gandhi acknowledged that civil disobedience may be dangerous, he considered it to be far less dangerous than violence which inevitably produces more violence. Noncooperation and civil disobedience provide nonviolent alternatives to the endless cycles of violent encounters.

KING: NONVIOLENCE AND *AGAPE*

The general theme of Gandhi's thought which struck a responsive chord in King after two years of study of evangelical liberalism and the social gospel was Gandhi's refusal to separate the spiritual and the secular, the religious and the ethical, and the individual and the social. Gandhi combined a deeply religious faith with an intense social involvement. He absorbed himself completely in an attempt to meet the needs of his people, and he devoted his entire mature life to public service at great personal sacrifice. Religion and service to humankind were synonymous in his thought. According to his view, service to humanity was the avenue to both self-realization and the experience of God.

Gandhi's blend of intense social involvement and mystical faith puzzled many people — some claiming he was essentially a saint trying to dabble in politics; others that he was really a politician using religion as a guise to accomplish his goals. The awareness of this ambiguous image led Gandhi to comment on one occasion: "Men say I am a saint losing myself in politics. The fact is that I am a politician trying my hardest to be a saint."[19] Gandhi seems to have sold himself short in this response, as some of his most perceptive interpreters have been quick to note. Louis Fischer, for example, seems to have the more accurate analysis when he concludes that for Gandhi the religious and the political were inseparable.

> The important fact is that in politics Gandhi always cleaved to religion and moral considerations, and as a saint he never thought his place was in a cave or cloister but rather in the hurly-burly of the popular struggle for rights and right. Gandhi's religion cannot be divorced from his politics. His religion made him political. His politics were religious.[20]

In the attempt to understand both Gandhi and King it is instructive to note that the term "prophet" has been applied consistently to those individuals who have actively striven to actualize their religious vision within the context of relational configurations of power. They have not been content to perform as "a voice crying in the wilderness." As the late Saul Alinsky was fond of saying, it is only those people who are "in there with it" who have the ability to see the forests *and* the trees. Mahatma Gandhi was surely such a person, and this was certainly not lost on Martin Luther King. We find the same blend of the religious and the social in King's life and writing.

Although King's religious presuppositions were drawn from Christian theology and ethics, his explication of nonviolence drew freely upon both the thought and example of Gandhi at the level of strategy and tactics. In order to understand King's interpretation of nonviolence, it is necessary to understand the options he saw open to an oppressed people in their struggle for social change. In his view, there were three major alternatives: resignation, violence, and nonviolent resistance.

The first option is *resignation* and *acquiescence*. Even though this response generally would be acknowledged as the easiest and least costly route to follow, King considered it to be immoral — the response of the coward. To submit passively to an oppressor simply reinforces the myth of racial superiority; moreover, it increases the oppressor's feeling of superiority and heightens his or her scorn. Resignation does not develop self-respect in the victim nor create respect for the oppressed in the mind of the oppressor. This kind of reasoning led King to affirm the Gandhian principle: "Noncooperation with evil is as much a moral obligation as is cooperation with good."[21] To acquiesce to an evil system is to say tacitly to the oppressor, "You are right and I agree with you." Over a period of time, the oppressor's conscience is numbed; he or she rationalizes the system as moral and becomes unsusceptible to appeals to ethics and justice. To combat this syndrome, King coined the slogan, "Never let them rest!" — an echo of the advice Gandhi had given his followers regarding the British during the Indian campaign for independence.

The second option open to an oppressed people in their

struggle for liberation is *physical violence*. It might appear in the short run that violence produces results, King observed, but this is an illusion because its so-called fruits are always temporary. Violence never permanently solves any problem; it simply produces new and more complex ones. Therefore, in King's mind, violence would be a futile street for blacks to travel in their struggle for racial justice because it is both impractical and immoral. It is impractical because "the eye-for-an-eye philosophy" leaves everybody blind. It is immoral because its goal is the humiliation of the opponents instead of their conversion. Violence annihilates relationships between people and groups that could make unity and community possible. Unity and community are impossible without communication. Violence feeds on hate instead of love; it seeks retaliation rather than reconciliation.

The third alternative King saw is *nonviolent resistance*. He viewed this alternative as a higher synthesis, combining the truths and avoiding the errors of the other options. By this he meant that the civil rights movement had rejected the acquiescence of the first option and the physical violence of the second option. That is to say, the nonviolent resister assumes that violent reaction should be avoided at all costs but that resistance must be made that goes beyond the "normal" political process. King might have read Reinhold Niebuhr's observation to arrive at this conclusion: "Even in a just and free society, there must be forms of pressure short of violence, but more potent than the vote, to establish justice in collective relations."[22] At any rate, King understood Niebuhr's reasoning: Persons in positions of power seldom, if ever, give up power without an all-out struggle.

One should not infer from this emphasis upon the need to go beyond the normal political process that King viewed nonviolent resistance as a substitute for the legal activity of the National Association for the Advancement of Colored People or the legislation of local, state, and national governments. But King was keenly aware from the lessons of history and his own experience that law, education, and the best intentions of people do not automatically bring about social change. Laws may be passed, but they must be obeyed to be effective; knowledge and education may simply provide people with "reasons" to defend their vested interests.

In spite of these reservations, no other subject appears more frequently in King's writings than the need for the federal government to enforce the laws of the land and to enact laws designed to prohibit segregation and discrimination.

> Let us never succumb to the temptation of believing that legislation and judicial decrees play only minor roles.... Morality cannot be legislated, but behavior can be regulated. Judicial decrees may not change the heart, but they can restrain the heartless. The law cannot make an employer love an employee, but it can prevent him from refusing to hire me because of the color of my skin. The habits, if not the hearts of people, have been and are being altered by legislative acts, judicial decisions, and executive orders. Let us not be misled by those who argue that segregation cannot be ended by force of law.[23]

King's emphasis upon law and legislation is significant because it indicates that he did not succumb to the anti-political bias frequently characteristic of exponents of nonviolence and pacifism. In King's mind, nonviolent resistance was not a substitute for sophisticated political analysis or the use of the mechanisms provided by the political process to achieve justice. He often referred to his strategy as "petition protest," a method of petitioning a government to correct injustices within the system, not a means of overthrowing the whole system.

The analysis of the assumptions of nonviolence does not occupy a prominent place in King's writings. The fullest and clearest account appears in *Stride Toward Freedom*. With the exception of a little-known article, "Love, Law and Civil Disobedience,"[24] wherein he did elaborate somewhat on the material in *Stride Toward Freedom*, all of the analyses of nonviolence in King's works are variations of the material in *Stride Toward Freedom*. In all of his works nonviolence is discussed in terms of six major principles or characteristics.

The first characteristic of nonviolent resistance is: It "is not a method for cowards; it does resist."[25] By this emphasis King is attempting to establish the fact that nonviolence involves courage, not cowardice, and that it is an active form of resistance, not "stagnant passivity." In support of this view King called Gandhi to his defense: "This is why Gandhi often said that if cowardice is the only alternative to violence, it is better to fight."[26] To be more specific, nonviolence is rooted in spiritual strength and personal courage. The practitioner of nonviolence pits one's entire being against the oppressor. There is nothing weak and submissive about this method; to the contrary, it is the method of the strong.

Advocates of violence find it difficult, if not impossible, to comprehend the courage requisite to nonviolent resistance as King conceived it. Even some exponents of nonviolence are unaware that for both Gandhi and King one must have the wherewithal to be violent before one can choose to be nonviolent. What Gandhi and King perceived is the vital connection between courage and both violence and nonviolence. They were quite clear that without courage one can be neither violent nor nonviolent. One must come to the point where he or she is not demoralized, self-deprecating, or impotent before one can choose to be nonviolent. One must have the strength and the will as well as the ability to kill before one can exhibit the supreme courage of choosing not to kill. One must at least become capable of violence before one can measure up to the stringent demands of nonviolence. Moral merit and power may be attributed only to one who has the strength and desire to be violent but who nevertheless demonstrates free choice by electing to be nonviolent. In short, courage and choice are the building blocks of nonviolent resistance.

King went to great lengths to make it quite clear that nonviolence is not passive but active; it is a dynamic way of resisting evil aspects of a social system. Following the lead of Gandhi and the criticisms of Reinhold Niebuhr, King questioned the validity of the phrase, "passive resistance," on the grounds that it connoted resignation and quietism. In order to press this point home, King repeatedly emphasized the great difference between "nonresistance" and "nonviolent resistance" to evil. He was well aware that much of the criticism leveled against nonviolence had been predicated on the failure to distinguish between the two concepts. Nonresistance leaves one stagnant, passive, and complacent; nonviolent resistance demands strong and determined resistance. In support of this position King often made the point that noncooperation with Jim Crow laws, demonstrations, and picketing, although negative in some respects, also had a positive side, that of the cooperation with the good and the constructive.

The second basic principle of nonviolent resistance is that "it does not seek to defeat or humiliate the opponent, but to win his friendship and understanding."[27] In this view, nonviolence is not a method of achieving change through physical force but a way of converting the opponent by demonstrating the justice of one's cause by the willingness to suffer for it. By this, King meant that nonviolence is a way of catching or drawing one's opponent off balance, hoping thereby to change the opponent's mind. Hence, the various expressions of nonviolent protest (i.e., boycotts, strikes, demonstrations, imprisonment, etc.) should not be viewed as ends per se but rather as tactics "to awaken a sense of moral shame in the opponent."[28] When nonviolent resistance is practiced effectively, it disarms the opponent, exposes moral defenses, weakens morale, and disturbs the conscience. Over a period of time the opponent will have had more adverse publicity than he or she can stand. "Forced to stand before the world and his God splattered with the blood of his brother, he will call an end to his self-defeating massacre."[29]

In the exposition of this aspect of nonviolent resistance, King reflects a debt to the concept of "moral jiu-jitsu" that Richard Gregg had expounded in *The Power of Nonviolence*, now a classic among advocates of nonviolence. Gregg had lived about four years in India (1925–1929), spending several months at Gandhi's *Sabarmati ashram*. According to his account, he made a careful study of all the written material available on Gandhi at that time.

The first edition of *The Power of Nonviolence* appeared in 1935; it was revised in 1944 (the edition King read at Crozer) and dedicated to Gandhi. After subsequent visits to India and in response to the growing civil rights movement in the South, Gregg issued a second revised edition in 1959 for which King wrote a very appreciative foreword. (This edition included an account of the Montgomery bus boycott and King's key role.)[30]

The essentials of "moral jiu-jitsu," reflecting the principles of the ancient sport in which balance is the key, may be summarized as follows: In physical jiu-jitsu the aim is to destroy the sense of balance in the opponent while retaining one's own balance. In moral jiu-jitsu the goal is to make the opponents lose their moral balance, thereby converting them to the position of nonviolent resisters. In order for moral jiu-jitsu to be successful, the victim must be willing to suffer, not to inflict suffering. If a blow is returned for a blow, the attacker is reassured and will feel that he or she has moral justification for the action. By retaliating, the victim thereby assigns violence to the same place on his or her "scale of values" as does the attacker. But if the victim chooses to suffer rather than to retaliate, the attacker loses the moral support which the usual violent resistance of most victims would render. "He plunges forward, as it were, into a new world of values."[31] Such an experience might result in a change in the outlook of the opponent; in fact, it can lead to a change of heart.

As a result of the exercise of moral jiu-jitsu, the attacker is surprised, loses poise, may become confused in his or her thinking, and is rendered incapable of action — in short, thrown off balance. In this new situation, the attacker's "instincts no longer tell him instantly what to do."[32] By way of contrast, the nonviolent resister is neither surprised nor weakened by anger; he or she is in firm control of self and actions. In this way, the victim achieves the upper hand by seizing the moral initiative. King provided an excellent example of how this process works by citing an incident that occurred in Birmingham, Alabama. A group of blacks had planned to have a prayer meeting near the city jail where a number of other blacks had been incarcerated. When they began to march to the jail, Bull Connor, the sheriff, told the police to turn the hoses on the marchers.

> What happened in the next thirty seconds was one of the most fantastic events of the Birmingham story. Bull Connor's men, their deadly hoses poised for action, stood facing the marchers. The marchers, many of them on their knees, stared back, unafraid and unmoving. Slowly the Negroes stood up and began to advance. Connor's men, as though hypnotized, fell back, their hoses sagging uselessly in their hands while several hundred Negroes marched past them without further interference, and held their prayer meeting as planned.[33]

The hope of nonviolent resistance is that the basis of fear and anger will be eliminated from the attacker's mind, and he or she will see the justice of the victim's position. King indicates that he thoroughly grasps Gregg's meaning of moral jiu-jitsu when, in answering a question about the meaning of "militant nonviolence," he responded:

> If you confront a man who has long been cruelly misusing you, and say, "Punish me, if you will, I do not deserve it, but I will accept it so that the world will know I am right and you are wrong," then you wield a powerful and a just weapon. This man, your oppressor, is automatically morally defeated, and if he has any conscience, he is ashamed. Wherever this weapon is used in a manner that stirs a community's or a nation's anguished conscience, then the pressure of public opinion becomes an ally in your just cause.[34]

But one should not infer from such statements that for King moral jiu-jitsu was simply a strategy for social change; it was also a fundamental assumption of his theology. In his mind, the goal of nonviolence is reconciliation.

Another principle of nonviolent resistance is: "The attack is directed against forces of evil rather than against persons who happen to be doing the evil."[35] King is quite clear that the issue is injustice and evil, not race or color. He affirmed this principle at the outset in Montgomery, and he never wavered from it as the movement progressed and his thought matured. (Gandhi, too, made a distinction between evil and the evildoer.) By the same token, a victory should not be construed in personal terms, but rather as a stride toward the advance of truth, love, and justice. This emphasis reflects King's deep awareness of the structural character of human life and the effect of social structures upon human personality. Individuals are victims of social structures and social institutions; structures, so to speak, structure relationships. In order to change relationships, it is necessary to change the structural arrangements of a social system.

The fourth characteristic of nonviolent resistance is "a willingness to accept suffering without retaliation, to accept blows from the opponent without striking back."[36] Nothing was more essential to King's thought than the willingness of the nonviolent resister to accept suffering as a testimony to the rightness of his or her cause. He even went so far as to measure one's degree of acceptance of nonviolence by the amount of suffering one was willing to endure. One must be willing to risk loss of house, unemployment, vilification of character, harassment by law officers and neighbors — even death. He reasoned that the sacrifice of self is infinitely superior to the sacrifice of others, and he saw sacrifice as the supreme manifestation of one's commitment to serve humankind. With this emphasis King plumbs the depths of nonviolence. He had learned from Gandhi that progress in the achievement of social justice, especially in matters like prejudice and racism, comes through suffering because it reaches beneath the rational and the conscious. Reason has to be enlightened by suffering; suffering is an aid to understanding.

There is obviously a relationship in King's mind between moral jiu-jitsu and the effect suffering has upon the viewers of the nonviolent resister. This is what King meant when he said: "Suffering ... has tremendous educational and transforming possibilities."[37] But over and above the tactical value of suffering, King affirmed it as a theological principle and related it to the cross of Jesus Christ — "unearned suffering is redemptive."[38] Suffering can save both black and white from a paralysis of the spirit. King was certain that suffering would sway relationships not only between individuals but also between nations and communities. He viewed the willingness to suffer rather than the wish to inflict suffering as the dynamic for the survival of Western civilization. It was also an essential ingredient of his vision of the Beloved Community.

A fifth characteristic of nonviolent resistance is that "it is based on the conviction that the universe is on the side of justice."[39] It has already been noted that a major theme of King's thought is the existence of a moral law of the cosmos that unfolds with the historical process. Or as he stated it: "There is a creative force in this universe that works to bring the disconnected aspects of reality into a harmonious whole."[40] This basic religious belief led him to affirm that the "universe is on the side of justice" and to the conviction that in the fight for freedom the protestor has "cosmic companionship."

The belief that God is on the side of those who struggle for justice allows the adherent of nonviolence, King believed, to have hope, to suffer and to sacrifice without striking back, and to persevere in the struggle for justice in spite of all obstacles. King noted with approval Thomas Jefferson's comment on his misgivings and fears about slavery in *Notes on Virginia*: "...I tremble for my country when I reflect that God is just, that his justice cannot sleep forever...the Almighty has no attribute which can take sides with us in such a contest."[41] Hence, King affirmed confidently that the civil rights movement has a faith in the future and that it would be victorious.

The sixth characteristic of nonviolent resistance is that "it avoids not only external physical violence but also internal violence of the spirit."[42] One should not retaliate with an attitude of hatred and bitterness any more than one should react with physical force, if one is a true nonviolent resister. By this, King meant that the norm of the Christian life is love. In the context of the explication of this sixth characteristic of nonviolence, he gave his fullest and clearest exposition of what he meant by love and why it is so central in the philosophy of nonviolent resistance. Whereas Gandhi's view of nonviolent resistance was rooted in *truth-force*, King's was rooted in *love-force*. By love King meant the Christian concept of *agape*, and this is why we have insisted upon the centrality of Christian theology and ethics. Furthermore, even a cursory reading of King's discussions of *agape* reveals a direct dependence upon Anders Nygren and Paul Ramsey. To understand King at this crucial point, it is necessary to relate the reason for King's dependence upon them.

During the spring term of King's senior year at Crozer Seminary (1951), he took a course, with one of the authors, on Christian ethics called "Christianity and Society." It was a study of "the social principles of Christianity and their bearing on contemporary life; the church as an institution and its relation to the social, political, and economic orders; analysis and interpretation of certain practical issues . . . war, racial prejudice, and world order."[43] In this course King studied systematically for the first time the biblical and theological bases, the norms and values of the Christian ethic.

Two basic texts were used: John Bennett's *Christian Ethics and Social Policy* and Paul Ramsey's *Basic Christian Ethics*. The texts were supplemented with Anders Nygren's *Agape and Eros*, Richard Niebuhr's *The Social Sources of Denominationalism*, and Liston Pope's *Millhands and Preachers*. The major written assignment, chosen to highlight the differences between the liberal and neo-Protestant approaches to Christian ethics, was a critical review of A. C. Knudson's *The Principles of Christian Ethics* (liberal) and Reinhold Niebuhr's *An Interpretation of Christian Ethics* (neo-Protestant). King attempted to combine the insights of both Ramsey and Nygren with Knudson to arrive at an interpretation of the Christian ethic which, if not unique, was certainly novel. He would agree with Ramsey that *agape* is the foundation of the Christian ethic and with Knudson that love is a natural capacity of every human being.

In his attempts to explain the rationale of the Montgomery bus boycott, he had spoken of love as the central theme of nonviolence, relying upon Jesus' saying, "Love your enemies." However, because King knew that people interpreted love in a variety of ways, he thought it was necessary to clarify what he meant. Thus he launched into a distinction between the three Greek words for love: *eros, philia,* and *agape.*[44] He concluded that only *agape* expressed what he had in mind when he spoke of loving one's enemies and oppressors because *agape* is completely self-giving and self-sacrificial. Christian love is "redeeming good will for all men. It is an overflowing love which is purely spontaneous, unmotivated, groundless, and creative. It is not set in motion by any quality or function of its object."[45] Nygren had written that "*agape* is spontaneous and 'unmotivated,'" "indifferent to value," "creative," and "the initiator of fellowship with God."[46] It is strange that King never mentions Nygren by name in any of his written works.

It is in the elaboration of the definition of *agape* that the influence of Paul Ramsey is unmistakable. By way of explanation, King wrote:

> *Agape* is disinterested love. It is a love in which the individual seeks not his own good, but the good of his neighbor (I Cor. 10:24). *Agape* does not begin by discriminating between worthy and unworthy people, or any qualities people possess. It begins by loving others *for their sakes.* It is an entirely "neighbor-regarding concern for others," which discovers the neighbor in every man it meets. Therefore, *agape* makes no distinction between friend and enemy; it is directed toward both.[47]
>
> Another basic point about *agape* is that it springs from the *need* of the other person — his need for belonging to the best in the human family. The Samaritan who helped the Jew on the Jericho Road was "good" because he responded to the human need that he was presented with.[48]

Ramsey begins chapter 3, "The Meaning of Christian Love," of *Basic Christian Ethics* with a discussion of Christian love as "disinterested love for neighbor" and refers at once to 1 Corinthians 10:24. Some of the phrases used in this chapter to describe disinterested love are: "love for another [neighbor] *for his own sake,*" it "discovers the neighbor in every man it meets and as such has never yet met a friend or an enemy," and "an entirely 'neighbor-regarding concern for others,'" which begins with the first man it sees."[49] Ramsey also uses the parable of the good Samaritan to illustrate his point by noting that the parable was not told to answer the abstract question, "Who is my neighbor?" but rather to explain the meaning of "neighborly love." For Ramsey, the neighbor includes the enemy; in fact, he coins the phrase "enemy-neighbor," and he points to such love as the epitome of *agape* because nothing can be expected in return. King's words on this subject are almost identical: "Consequently, the best way to assure oneself that love is disinterested is to have love for the enemy-neighbor from whom you can expect no good in return, but only hostility and persecution."[50]

One of the major themes of Ramsey, elaborated on in an entire chapter on "The Work of Christian Love," is the relationship between *agape* and the creation and preservation of community. "Only an element of concern for the other person *for his own sake*," he notes, "creates community among men."[51] A community may be preserved by many things, including self-love, mutual love, enlightened self-interest, or even force, but only *agape* can create community where none has ever existed. Only Christian love can take a broken human situation and bring healing and reconciliation.

In explaining further his own analysis, King also links *agape* with the attempt to originate and to maintain community. He speaks of *agape* as "love in action," "love seeking to preserve and create community," "a willingness to go to any length to restore community," and as "the only cement that can hold this broken community together."[52] He relates *agape* to the cross of Jesus Christ and finds here "the eternal expression of the length to which God will go to restore broken community."[53] The connection made between love and community was an element of one of King's fundamental theological assumptions: all life is a part of a single process; all human beings are brothers and sisters. One cannot do good or harm to another person without both parties being affected. King's deeply held belief in the organic unity of life is symbolized by his frequent use of John Donne's theme, "No man is an island." In this understanding of love and his faith in its efficacy, we find the cornerstone of King's vision of the Beloved Community.

It would be misleading to leave King's views on Christian love in this form without noting that he disagreed with Nygren and Ramsey about a very crucial theological issue. In the tradition of Nygren and Ramsey, *agape* had always been understood in terms of God's love at work in the human heart. Nygren stressed, for example, that we are to love our neighbor because God has loved us. It follows that God's love for us and our love for the neighbor is not based on "the infinite value of the human soul."[54] Such a view would preclude the value-creating role of *agape* and make unnecessary a decision on the part of God to love people.

In Ramsey's view, *agape* is a theological ultimate, and it cannot be defined by non-Christian categories. *Agape* is God's standard, not people's; it is irreducible to human terms. The source of Christian love is "God's righteousness and love," and it is not to be found elsewhere "in some moral norms derived from reason operating apart from the Hebrew-Christian religious heritage." In other words, *agape* is "a supernatural measure," a norm "radically different from any other which has commended itself to the human mind."[55] This means that the neighbor is not loved because he or she has inherent worth but because loving is God's will. "Christian love ... does not rest upon a doctrine of the infinite, inherent value of human personality. ... "[56]

King recoiled from this aspect of the Nygren-Ramsey view because it ran crosswise to Davis's liberalism and Brightman's personalism. Liberalism and personalism had affirmed a belief in the inherent dignity and worth of human personality. Hence, certain questions were raised in King's mind about the Nygren-Ramsey position: Does it not raise the Christian ethic above the range of human experience? Is it not indifferent to the structures of human ability and need? Would God require what is basically unrelated to human nature? King refused to accept the idea that human dignity is only derived; to the contrary, it had to be inherent if people were to be moral agents. He insisted:

There must be a recognition of the sacredness of human personality. Deeply rooted in our political and religious heritage is the conviction that every man is an heir to a legacy of dignity and worth.... This innate worth referred to in the phrase *image of God* is universally shared in equal portion by all men.[57]

Hence, King denied that Christians are mere channels of God's love. Since God's love is an act, the same must be true of our love for our fellow human beings.

In spite of the fact that the rejection of this aspect of the Nygren-Ramsey position seems to indicate that King was trying to ride two horses traveling in opposite directions, it is true, nevertheless, that King endorsed the liberal position of Knudson at this point. In his review of Knudson's *The Principles of Christian Ethics* and Niebuhr's *An Interpretation of Christian Ethics,* he agreed with Knudson that there was a fatal flaw in the Nygren-Ramsey position. Speaking specifically of the *agape* theory expounded by Nygren, Knudson wrote:

In so far as this theory completely eliminates moral worth from the objects of the divine grace and in so far as it entirely excludes duties to self from the Christian ethic, it de-moralizes and de-personalizes the Christian life. It leaves both the divine grace and the law of brotherly love without a rational basis. Blind faith takes the place of moral insight. We affirm the divine love and the duty of brotherly love, but without any rational ground for either.[58]

Beginning with this assumption, Knudson goes on to say that Nygren's position must be supplemented with the affirmation of "the moral nature of man" and "his endowment with a native moral capacity.... Indeed, this belief is the basal assumption of all true morality."[59] By moral nature, Knudson meant people's "capacity for moral experience" which is "due to a native capacity of the human spirit, a capacity to distinguish between right and wrong, to form ideals, and to govern one's actions accordingly."[60] Knudson adds that one of our native moral capacities is love because "...the principle of love...is inherent in the normal interaction of moral beings...."[61]

It is clear that Knudson's interpretation of the moral nature of humans was significantly indebted to Immanuel Kant's "moral categorical imperative," as had been the case for liberalism in general. King undoubtedly understood this influence very well since he had taken a whole semester's course on Kant at the University of Pennsylvania during the year just prior to his study of Knudson.[62] But in this view *agape* becomes little more than the altruism of "natural" ethics. This is obvious not only in King's ethics but also in his Christology in which Jesus becomes the symbol of what all people may become, the example all should and can emulate. The love exemplified by the cross of Jesus is viewed as the epitome of the cosmic process, and every human being, as a product of this process, has the capacity to actualize love in his or her relations with others. Martin Luther King's faith that all people would respond to nonviolence was rooted in the liberal tenet that all humans have an innate moral capacity which, when activated by love, will compel them to respond in a similar fashion.

To whatever degree King may have modified some aspects of liberalism, primarily as a result of the influence of Reinhold Niebuhr (see chapter 4), he seems to have retained the liberal view that love is a simple historical possibility, applicable not only in interpersonal relations but in group relations as well. It is generally agreed that this had been the social gospel position on the relationship between love and social policy. Edward Long has made the apt observation:

> This optimism [i.e., of the social gospel] was not measured by the lack of a conception of sin in the theology of the movement. The leaders of the social gospel [e.g., Walter Rauschenbusch] knew the power of sin and bravely castigated those who were making private gain at social expense. The optimism of the social gospel was apparent, rather, in its trust that Christian love could be translated into social reality without a process of compromise.[63]

Although King's thought was somewhat more complicated than that of the social gospel, especially in the sense that love and justice were not identified, Long's explanation helps us to understand how King could agree with Reinhold Niebuhr about "the complexity of man's social involvement and the glaring reality of collective evil"[64] and still advocate the efficacy of nonviolent resistance as the only acceptable Christian method of social change.

Martin Luther King, taking many of his cues from Gandhi's thought and activity, considered both noncooperation and civil disobedience to be tactical manifestations of nonviolent resistance. However, King's presuppositions for these tactics of nonviolent resistance were not derived from Gandhi but from the tradition of Israel's prophets and the early Christians. To be more exact, King often cited the First Commandment and Peter's affirmation in Acts 5:29, "We must obey God rather than men."

King was forced during the early days of the boycott in Montgomery to choose between the long-standing traditions of that community and the moral imperatives of the Christian ethic as he conceived them. "As Christians," he announced with assurance, "we own our ultimate allegiance to God and His will, rather than to man and his folkways."[65] Here is the prophetic principle of Rauschenbusch in which absolute loyalty is given to God alone and not to any historical relativity, whether it be a race, a class, a state, or a nation. King knew that adherence to this principle would inevitably bring him into conflict not only with social custom but also with state and national laws. But King did not hesitate to press forward because he was convinced that in order to be true to the moral demands of the God of the Christian faith, one had no choice under certain circumstances but to refuse to cooperate with immoral laws of a social system.

King's most explicit statement of the argument for civil disobedience is found in his famous distinction between a "just" and an "unjust" law. As this distinction indicates, King assumed that there are two kinds of laws, and he saw the difference in terms of the natural law tradition of Western philosophy: "A just law is a man-made code that squares with the moral law or the law of God. An unjust law is a code that is out of harmony with moral law."[66] In more explicit theological terms, a just law, using the language of Thomas Aquinas, is a human law that embodies eternal and natural law while an unjust law does not.

In practical terms this distinction between a just and an unjust law meant that a law is just or unjust depending upon whether it elevates or debases human personality, whether it contributes to or impedes the growth of the human person. In support of this position, King proudly cited St. Augustine's famous dictum, "An unjust law is no law at all." Thus King did not hesitate to insist that the goals of the civil rights movement were not only right, legally and constitutionally speaking, but also that they were in accordance with the will of God. While Christians are both legally and morally obligated to obey a just law, they also have a moral responsibility to disobey an unjust law.

On the basis of whether a law met the requirements stipulated above, King decided whether a law was just or unjust. His criterion was not simply "legality"; it was also justice and morality. A law that embodies the latter, one gladly obeys. If a law does not embody justice and morality, one disobeys it hoping to change it. At no time, then, was King disrespectful of the law per se. He never advocated indiscriminate evasion or defiance of law in general. He agreed with Gandhi that such an approach would lead to anarchy. On the other hand, when King was confronted with a law which he considered to be clearly unjust, he felt morally compelled to disobey it and to accept the penalty prescribed.

It seems, therefore, that King stands in the tradition of the classical understanding of civil disobedience: Out of obedience to a higher law (God), one should follow the dictates of one's conscience and gladly break an unjust law. But out of respect for the human-made laws of the state, one should accept the consequences of one's act. Consequently, jail became an important symbol for King as it had been for Gandhi. In the early days of the Montgomery bus boycott, King was obviously happy when convicted by a local court because it not only symbolized a deep identification with blacks suffering from segregation but also pointed out a breach of an unjust law. He remembered that he felt guilty only of "the crime of desiring for my people the inalienable rights of life, liberty, and the pursuit of happiness."[67] As the movement grew and more and more people were incarcerated, King observed that imprisonment became a badge of honor proudly worn because it symbolized to blacks a new sense of human dignity. In King's words: "He was *somebody*. He had a sense of *somebodiness*. He was *impatient* to be free."[68]

CHAPTER FOUR

Reinhold Niebuhr: Sin and Power

I N ADDITION TO THOSE influences already discussed, there were others during King's senior year at Crozer Seminary that would be significant for his thought. "My intellectual odyssey to nonviolence," King wrote, "did not end here [i.e., Gandhi]. During my last year in theological school, I began to read the works of Reinhold Niebuhr."[1] This part of King's intellectual pilgrimage took place in two courses on Christian ethics, "Christianity and Society," already mentioned in chapter 3, and "Christian Social Philosophy II." The latter was the second part of a two-term course on the history of Christian ethics from Immanuel Kant to 1950; however, the major portion was devoted to an analysis and critical comparison of liberalism (Rauschenbusch) and Christian realism (Reinhold Niebuhr).[2]

King studied Reinhold Niebuhr for the first time in "Christian Social Philosophy II." He also returned to the study of Rauschenbusch, but this time around he saw Rauschenbusch in juxtaposition to Niebuhr. Although King would vacillate back and forth in reaction to certain aspects of Niebuhr's thought, it is not going too far to say that King was never again comfortable with certain emphases of liberalism after his introduction to the thought of Reinhold Niebuhr. He admitted readily that his first encounter with Niebuhr's *Moral Man and Immoral Society,* one of the few books mentioned by title in King's writings and the only one mentioned more frequently than Rauschenbusch's *Christianity and the Social Crisis,*[3] left him "confused" and later on that he "began to question some of the theories that had been associated with so-called liberal theology."[4] Finally, he confessed that he "became so enamored of his [Niebuhr's] social ethics that I almost fell into the trap of accepting uncritically everything he wrote."[5] In short, Niebuhr burst like a bombshell into King's liberal theological-ethical world view. King's testimony to Reinhold Niebuhr should not be interpreted to mean that he abandoned evangelical liberalism and accepted Niebuhrianism. He would always remain essentially an evangelical liberal and a personalist. He would never abandon liberalism's emphasis upon the role of reason in theological reflection, the value of biblical criticism for the interpretation of Scripture, and other liberal tenets to be discussed later. The testimony to Niebuhr means, rather, that his arguments against certain aspects of liberalism were so persuasive that King could not be intellectually honest with himself and ignore them. The truth is that King would incorporate many of Niebuhr's insights into his mature thought, although the attempt to do so raised tensions in his thought that remained unresolved at the time of his death.

However, King's interpreters have paid very little attention, in most cases none, to those tenets of Niebuhr which had a significant impact upon King's thought — a gross error, considering not only King's own words but also the observation of Andrew J. Young, a former executive secretary of the Southern Christian Leadership Conference and one of King's key tacticians. Young said in a speech at a testimonial dinner for John Bennett:

> I want to begin by saying that there was always a misunderstanding of what Martin Luther King was about. I remember one night when somebody came at him with some of the philosophical presuppositions of strict Gandhian nonviolence, and he responded about three o'clock in the morning with the most brilliant lecture I had every heard on *The Nature and Destiny of Man*, Reinhold Niebuhr, and the thinking of John Bennett and *Christianity and Crisis*. He reminded us that he had done his Ph.D. thesis on Paul Tillich, and you realized how everything he did was formulated much more out of a sense of Christian realism and out of the historic Black reality of the Christian Church in the Southern part of the United States than I think the press ever really understood.

We always tried to make nonviolence something that was very idealistic and ethereal and for the saints to live by, and never really understood, as Dr. Niebuhr said as far back as *Moral Man and Immoral Society*, that nonviolent power and economic withdrawal would be the means that the Black community might eventually use to gain justice.[6]

While some of the language of Young may be somewhat exaggerated, he is essentially correct that no account of the intellectual sources of Martin Luther King would be adequate without a thorough analysis of the influence of Reinhold Niebuhr.

REINHOLD NIEBUHR AND CHRISTIAN REALISM

Scholars in the field of the development of theology in the United States generally acknowledge that the publication of *Moral Man and Immoral Society* (1932) by Reinhold Niebuhr (1892–1971) marked the beginning of the decline of liberalism and the ascendancy of Christian realism as the dominant school of theology in the United States.* After the publication of Niebuhr's *Moral Man and Immoral Society* and *Reflections on the End of an Era* (1934), an increasing number of American theologians, who had also become familiar with developments in Europe, began to react critically to some of the content and most of the fruit of Protestant liberalism. The men most often associated with the reaction against liberalism are John Coleman Bennett, Walter Marshall Horton, Robert Lowry Calhoun, H. Richard Niebuhr, and Reinhold Niebuhr. All of them began to call, in their own way, for a radical "reconstruction" of liberal theology.

The word "reconstruction" is used advisedly: the neoorthodox movement, represented primarily by Karl Barth and Emil Brunner on the continent, was a more severe reaction to liberalism

---

*The term used by the exponents of the new position was "Christian realism." It is a more appropriate term than neoorthodoxy because, though many of the emphases were similar, there was a great deal of difference between the "Christian realism" of Niebuhr and the "neoorthodoxy" of Karl Barth and others.

than the thought of Reinhold Niebuhr. The American reaction, called "Christian realism" or "realistic theology," had some affinity with "the theology of crisis" of Barth and Brunner, especially in the areas of faith and reason, nature and grace, and a renewed appreciation of the revelation of God in Christ. However, Christian realism was a more moderate reaction to liberalism than neoorthodoxy in that Christian realism retained a far greater concern for social ethics. The distinction between neoorthodoxy and Christian realism did not escape Martin Luther King who wrote:

> Niebuhr's great contribution to contemporary theology is that he has refuted the false optimism characteristic of a great segment of Protestant liberalism, without falling into the anti-rationalism of the continental theologian Karl Barth, or the semi-fundamentalism of other dialectical theologians.[7]

The exponents of Christian realism argued that the biblical understanding of human nature, symbolized by the myth of the Fall, is a far more accurate, more realistic, understanding of the human situation than either the pessimism of Christian orthodoxy or the optimism of Christian liberalism. The one objective and empirically verifiable base, from which most realistic theologians operated because they thought it could be clearly documented as a fact of human experience, was the doctrine of original sin (i.e., the egoistic predicament of every human being). In short, Christian realism was the theological expression of a general revolt against the romanticism, the idealism, and the liberalism of the nineteenth century. Reinhold Niebuhr was the moving spirit of theological realism. Martin Luther King was an heir of this new school of thought through the influence of Reinhold Niebuhr.

HUMANITY: IMAGE OF GOD AND SINNER

The cardinal doctrine of Christian realism was its interpretation of human nature. When Martin Luther King said that after

studying Reinhold Niebuhr he "began to question some of the
theories that had been associated with the so-called liberal theology," he was referring principally to Niebuhr's critique of the
optimistic doctrine of humankind of Protestant liberalism. King
argued:

> Niebuhr has extraordinary insight into human nature, especially
> the behavior of nations and social groups....His theology is a
> persistent reminder of the reality of sin on every level of man's
> existence....While I still believed in man's potential for good,
> Niebuhr made me realize his potential for evil as well.[8]

King questioned liberalism primarily at the point of its view of
human nature, and he did so with grateful acknowledgment to
Niebuhr. To understand why this was true, it is necessary to
sketch Niebuhr's doctrine of humanity, highlighting his emphasis
upon the prevalence of the egoistic impulse in every person.

According to Niebuhr, human nature is best understood in
dialectical and paradoxical terms. That is, human nature is characterized by a constant tension between one's essential (i.e.,
created) nature and one's existential (i.e., self-determined) character — an ever-present conflict between good and evil impulses.
Hence, in *The Nature and Destiny of Man* Niebuhr begins his
exposition of the nature of human nature with the observation that humankind is "a problem to himself." Furthermore,
he contends that modern systems of thought, such as idealism,
naturalism, rationalism, and romanticism, have failed to explain
satisfactorily the source of the human predicament. The failure has resulted from the fact that modern systems of thought
have not dealt adequately with the three most important subjects related to the nature of human nature: (1) the relationship
between spirit (i.e., vitality) and nature (i.e., form); (2) the nature of individuality; and (3) the origin of evil. Niebuhr argued
that the Hebraic-Christian (biblical) view of human nature provides the most satisfactory answer to all three subjects. It explains
the first with the doctrine of *imago dei* (image of God); the
second with the concept of creaturehood; and the third with

the doctrine of original sin. These tenets, for Niebuhr, distinguish the Christian doctrine of human nature from all other alternatives.[9]

Image of God

According to the Christian faith as Niebuhr views it, the source of human uniqueness, that which distinguishes people from all other created objects, is that humans were created in the image of God. In this view, God is the creator of the world and everything therein. As "the crown of creation," humankind must be seen, therefore, from "the standpoint of God, rather than the uniqueness of his rational faculties or his relation to nature."[10] People are, to be sure, a part of nature, and their most distinctive characteristic is their capacity for rational thought. However, these facets of human nature are not the source of our uniqueness. The source of our uniqueness is the concept of *imago dei*, which Niebuhr defined in terms of our capacity for infinite self-transcendence. "It is the quality of the human spirit," he wrote, " ... to lift itself above itself as a living organism and to make the whole temporal and spatial world, including itself, the object of its knowledge."[11]

The principal faculties which permit the self to transcend its locus in time and space are *memory* and *imagination*. Through the use of memory, people can detach themselves from their immediate socio-cultural context to look at the past in all of its manifold aspects and to profit from both the wisdom and the folly of the past. Through the use of imagination, humans can transcend their immediate desires in order to consider the wishes of others and to plan for the future. In short, the capacity for self-transcendence enables one to criticize self, values, and institutions in light of universal values and to transform them in terms of transcendent norms. We are self-determining because we are able to transcend natural processes and to choose between alternatives. Not being subject to the determinism of the cause-and-effect scheme of nature, we are able to determine within limits our own end and destiny. In Niebuhr's thought, the capacity for infinite self-transcendence is synonymous with what is commonly called the spiritual dimension of human nature.

Creaturehood

In spite of the capacity for self-transcendence (i.e., spiritual nature), humans are also a part of nature. The *spirit* resides in a *body* which occupies a particular locus in space and time. The import of this fact is that a human is a *creature*, subject to the laws of the natural world. This is the case to such an extent that even at its best, the self remains a finite self. There is a sense then in which the self, though free, is also limited and bound. People are finite creatures because they are a part of nature.

To say that humans are finite does not mean that creaturehood is evil; it simply means that people are people and not God. Far from being evil, creatureliness is an essential aspect of our individuality, and it is essentially good. Niebuhr summarizes:

> In its purest form the Christian view of man regards man as a unity of God-likeness and creatureliness in which he remains a creature even in the highest spiritual dimensions of his existence and may reveal elements of the image of God even in the lowliest aspects of his natural life.[12]

Humans are a combination of spirit and nature, and we are subject to the demands of both. The unity of spirit (i.e., vitality) and nature (i.e., form) is the basis of our capacity for indeterminate possibilities for creative endeavors. Among these is the ability to construct communities characterized by freedom, justice, and peace. In political life it is this capacity which makes democracy possible.

Sin

God-likeness and creaturehood do not encompass all of the characteristics of human nature — people are also sinners. Sin is rooted, for Niebuhr, in the complex and paradoxical character of human nature. As a result of the capacity for self-transcendence, a human being is free; as a part of nature, a human being is also bound. In other words, humankind is a paradox of freedom and necessity. This paradoxical condition, free yet bound, makes us continuously subject to anxiety. However, anxiety is not sin; it is rather the precondition of sin. As a result of anxiety, people put the self at the center of the universe and everything therein. Thus we fall into an egocentric predicament, characterized by love of self instead of love of God. Pride (*hubris*) in our capacity for self-transcendence tempts us to absolutize our contingent existence.

Niebuhr's argument assumes that since humans were created in the image of God, the human principle of self-determination should be the will of God. If this principle of self-determination is anything other than the will of God, such as a self, a class, a race, or a nation, our essentially good nature will not be actualized but distorted. In other words, we deny our essence when we attribute ultimate significance to any provisional object or structure. One's attempt to absolutize the relative denies one's finitude and dependence upon God. Thus sin is not the result of human finitude but of the refusal to accept the limitations imposed by creaturehood. Niebuhr called humankind's revolt against the sovereignty of God the theological dimension of sin or original sin.

In Niebuhr's thought, sin also has an ethical dimension: the love of self to the exclusion of God (original sin) leads to the love of self to the exclusion of other selves (actual sins). In interpersonal and social relations one seeks to overcome anxiety and to achieve security by attempting to subordinate other selves to one's will by resorting to the unrestrained use of power. To be more specific, humankind's sinful nature is manifested in overt acts of injustice. Furthermore, the egoism of social groups is always greater than the egoism of individuals because a social group is less merciful, compassionate, and benevolent than an individual.

Actual sins become a structural aspect of social institutions, and injustice is perpetuated by social structure. This is the way injustice becomes a permanent factor in human society and why it is so difficult to eradicate. This is the reason it is proper to speak of institutionalized greed or racism or sexism. Since sin has a structural character, it is a constant in human life, not a variable which can be eliminated by love or education. When one's sinful nature is expressed in social relations, the community is disrupted and the common good is subverted. Hence, restraints have to be imposed upon the egoistic impulses of both individuals and groups through laws. According to Niebuhr's classic axiom: "Man's capacity [self-transcendence] for justice makes democracy possible; but man's inclination to injustice [egoism] makes democracy necessary."[13] It is clear that Niebuhr's doctrine of humanity qualified significantly the optimistic view of human nature that King had found in liberalism and the social gospel and that he had accepted uncritically for some time.

Martin Luther King's analysis of the nature of humanity employed a dialectical method of reasoning, rejecting the either/or in favor of the both/and approach. The dialectical method is employed in two different contexts with the same results. In one place, King contrasted liberalism and neoorthodoxy; in another place, he contrasted humanism and materialism. While King rejected certain aspects of liberalism's view of humanity, he could not unconditionally accept the tenets of neoorthodoxy. He considered liberalism too optimistic because of its overemphasis upon humanity's essential goodness, and neoorthodoxy too pessimistic because of its overemphasis upon humanity's essential evil.* "An

---

*For some reason King persists in many places in identifying Niebuhr with neoorthodoxy, though he makes it clear in other places that he is aware that Niebuhr should not be stereotyped in that way. This confusion often makes it difficult to analyze King's reaction to Niebuhr because King appears to be inconsistent. To charge Niebuhr with pessimism as King does in some places reveals a lack of appreciation of the dialectical nature of Niebuhr's thought. We have already seen that since Niebuhr placed a great deal of emphasis upon humanity's capacity for infinite self-transcendence, he believed that people have indeterminate possibilities for creative endeavors. However, there was development in King's thought regarding Niebuhr. King expressed a different attitude toward Niebuhr in *Strength to Love* and *Where Do We Go from Here: Chaos or Community?* than in *Stride Toward Freedom*. The reader should be aware of the development in King's attitude toward Niebuhr when he reads King's writings. While the early writings are characterized by criticisms and negative reactions, all the references to Niebuhr in King's writings during the latter part of King's career (1963–1968) are positive.

adequate understanding of man," he concluded, "is found neither in the thesis of liberalism nor in the antithesis of neoorthodoxy, but in a synthesis which reconciles the truths of both."[14]

In a sermon called "What Is Man?" King contrasted the pessimism of materialism and the optimism of humanism, and he found both to be inadequate. He agreed with another group of thinkers, later identified as Christian realists

> who, seeking to be a little more realistic about man, wish to reconcile the truths of these opposites [pessimism and optimism], while avoiding the extremes of both. They contend that the truth about man is found neither in the thesis of pessimistic materialism nor the antithesis of optimistic humanism, but in a larger synthesis.[15]

King called his synthesis "a realistic Christian view of man."[16] His debt to Niebuhr's *Nature and Destiny of Man* becomes very obvious in the categories used to explain "a realistic Christian view of man."

The most important characteristic of human nature for King is that a human is *a spiritual being made in the image of God.* He locates the essence of humanity's spiritual nature in the faculties of reason, memory, imagination, and freedom. Since people are free, they are able "to deliberate, to make decisions, and to choose between alternatives."[17] In other words, we have the capacity to determine our own destiny. As a result of the faculties of memory and imagination, we are able to transcend the limitations of nature and of time and space and to accomplish an infinite variety of creative things. As examples, King points to our abilities to write poetry and other literary works, to paint great masterpieces of art, and to create stirring compositions of music.

A human is not only a spiritual being, according to King, he or she is also a part of nature. People exhibit many of the same characteristics as all other animals, and they are subject to many of the same limitations. However, since God created us that way and because everything God created is good, the body is good — not evil and the source of sin. The view of the human body as evil, in King's view, is based upon the false analogy derived from

Greek philosophy wherein the soul is good and the body is evil. King supported his position by noting that such a dichotomy is not found in the Bible; rather, the biblical view sees the human as a unit, a whole constituted of body (matter) and soul (spirit). Christianity does not locate evil in the body or matter but in the will. (That is a Niebuhrian statement if ever there was one.) On the basis of such presuppositions, King consistently went on to argue that the Christian church should be concerned with *physical* as well as *spiritual* needs. It is true, King agrees, that "man does not live by bread alone," but it is equally true that he cannot live without it. Any version of the Christian faith that stresses "pie-in-the-sky-by-and-by" and neglects daily physical needs is a truncated and potentially dangerous version of Christianity.

In typical Niebuhrian fashion, King, having affirmed that humans are a composite of nature and spirit, rounded out his doctrine of humanity by concluding that people are sinners in need of the grace of God. It does not follow that since we are made in the image of God we will always actualize the potentialities of our created nature. The truth is, King regretfully observed, that it is not unusual for one to follow that dimension of one's nature inclined toward evil. King recognized that modern humanity does not like the word "sin" and either ignores it or uses other words to describe the egoistic side of human nature. But no matter what terms we use, the fact is that our acts are often corrupted by selfishness and the will to power. This is often the case even for those people who seem to have the highest motives and intentions. In a passage which reminds us of Niebuhr's discourse on spiritual pride, King wrote: "You must come to see that a man may be self-centered in his self-denial and self-righteous in his self-sacrifice. His generosity may feed his ego and his piety, his pride. Without love, benevolence becomes egotism and martyrdom becomes spiritual pride."[18]

One can hardly avoid the conclusion on the basis of this analysis that King's doctrine of humanity was stated precisely in the dialectical manner for which Reinhold Niebuhr is so well known. We humans are a walking bundle of paradoxes — even when we know what we ought to do, we do not do it. We often choose falsehood instead of truth, injustice instead of justice, hate rather than love. The barbarism humankind has perpetrated at times through wars and racial oppression is not even found among other animals. There seems to be a fatal flaw in human nature, according to King, that should never be forgotten: "Man is a sinner in need of God's forgiving grace. This is not deadening pessimism; it is Christian realism."[19]

One of the aspects of Niebuhr's view of evil that influenced King was what Niebuhr called "the historicity of reason," meaning that there is no unprejudiced mind and no person is devoid of pride. Human reasoning is always tainted with self-interest, and reason tends to serve the egoistic impulse. "The will-to-power," Niebuhr explains, "uses reason, as kings use courtiers and chaplains to add grace to their enterprise. Even the most rational men are never quite rational when their own interests are at stake."[20] There is no theme more prominent in Niebuhr's writings than the facility with which privileged groups seek to defend "rationally" (i.e., to rationalize) their privileged position. Since inequalities of privilege cannot be defended rationally, the privileged must be extraordinarily subtle and clever in "inventing specious proofs for the theory that universal values spring from, and that general interests are served by, the special privileges which they hold."[21]

From Niebuhr's analysis of the human egoistic predicament, King learned that reason may serve vested interests, be conditioned by social status, and be distorted by human sin. King wrote:

> I...came to see that the superficial optimism of liberalism concerning human nature overlooked the fact that reason is darkened by sin. The more I thought about human nature, the more I saw how our tragic inclination for sin encourages us to rationalize our actions. Liberalism failed to show that reason by itself is little more than an instrument to justify man's defensive ways of thinking. Reason, devoid of the purifying power of faith, can never free itself from distortions and rationalizations.[22]

As he grappled with the problem of the historicity of reason, King focused upon the position of the white liberal as an
excellent illustration. He referred to white liberals as innocent
children of light, a phrase obviously adopted from Niebuhr's *Children of Light and Children of Darkness.* King admitted reluctantly
that his most troublesome adversaries were not the Ku Klux
Klan or someone like Senator Eastland, the unabashed children
of darkness. Their prejudices were clearly visible and their position well-known; they could be dealt with in an open and honest
way. However, white liberals presented quite another problem because they often seemed oblivious to latent prejudice. As King
saw the situation, the stance of white liberals often leads to tokenism instead of equality because their advocacy of the cause
of minority groups often seems to be an expression of pride. By
way of contrast, King was impressed with the eloquence with
which segregationists stated their case, and he was amazed that
" 'the children of darkness' are frequently more determined and
jealous than the 'children of light.' "[23] He conjectured that the
timidity of the children of light helped to explain why structures of evil are so tenacious and fall so slowly. Thus, if time
is not used constructively to resist evil, it might continue to exist
indefinitely.

The analysis of King's interpretation of human nature shows
that it agrees substantially with the Christian realism of Reinhold
Niebuhr. The one qualification which needs to be made is a difference in emphasis which led King to come down at a somewhat
different place regarding the possibilities of the historical actualization of an inclusive human community. King insisted that
"there is within human nature an amazing potential for goodness."[24] He did not mean by this that humanity is basically good
as liberalism had held. He admitted that there is "a strange dichotomy of disturbing dualism" within human nature, and he
used Plato's charioteer, Ovid, Augustine, and Carlyle to docu-
ment this internal conflict within the human personality. King
meant, rather, "that man is neither innately good nor is he innately bad; he has potentialities for both."[25] Jesus and Gandhi

might appeal to the goodness in humanity and Hitler might appeal to the evil side. Be this as it may,

> we must never forget that there is something within human nature that can respond to goodness, that man is not totally depraved, to put it in theological terms, the image of God is never totally gone . . . there is something within human nature that can be changed, and this stands at the top of . . . the philosophy of non-violence.[26]

As the above statements suggest, King placed his major emphasis upon humanity's potentiality for goodness, and this was the source of his optimism about the successful outcome of the struggle for civil rights. In other words, the one major weakness King found in Niebuhr was his inability "to deal adequately with the *relative* perfection which is the fruit of the Christian life."[27] For King this meant that Niebuhr did not deal satisfactorily with the possibilities of spiritual growth, Christian values in personality, and how *agape* is actually realized in human nature and history. King explained by quoting Walter Muelder's criticism of Niebuhr:

> There is a Christian perfectionism which may be called a prophetic meliorism. . . . Niebuhr's treatment of much historical perfectionism is well-founded criticism from an abstract ethical viewpoint, but it hardly does justice to the constructive historical contributions of the perfectionist sects within the Christian fellowship and even within the secular order. There is a kind of Christian assurance which releases creative energy into the world and which in actual fellowship rises above the conflicts of individual and collective egoism.[28]

This aspect of King's doctrine of humanity, in spite of other evidence to the contrary, supported his optimism regarding the possibility of actualizing the Beloved Community. At the same time, Niebuhr's stress upon human sin and egoism influenced significantly King's views on the uses and abuses of power in collective human life and the tactics required to make the Beloved Community an actuality.

Power, Justice, and Love

In speaking of his debt to Reinhold Niebuhr, King made special note of the fact that Niebuhr was "keenly aware of the complexity of human motives and of the relation between morality and power."[29] Niebuhr's insights on these subjects led King "to recognize the complexity of man's social involvement and the glaring reality of collective evil."[30] In the thought of both Niebuhr and King, the analysis of the relationship between ethics, power, and politics was always intertwined with their views on the relationship between love and justice. Power, justice, and love were always interrelated in their theology and ethics, and it is impossible to discuss one of them in isolation from the others. Reinhold Niebuhr's belief in the prevalence of the egoistic impulse in every person led him to emphasize the need for a realistic understanding of the uses and abuses of power. Niebuhr began his discussion of the relationship between morality and power by observing that relationships between social groups are basically political, not ethical, because social relations are determined more by how much power each group possesses than by the moral claims of each group. In other words, the issue in most social conflicts is the possession or lack of power. Social inequity is the result, not of the failure of religious and rational people to act more lovingly and reasonably, but the possession of an inordinate amount of power by a particular social group or class. The concentration of power in one social group leads to the entrenchment of power, and power automatically gives that group a privileged position and an advantage over other groups.

When it came to explaining why privileged classes always resist change, Niebuhr responded unequivocally that it is due to the fact that they are the beneficiaries of social injustice. For another thing, power always continues to exploit weakness until it is challenged by countervailing power. Social groups with power, property, and privilege do not voluntarily relinquish any of their advantages; to the contrary, advantages have to be wrested from them. Even earnest appeals and moral suasion are not sufficient weapons against entrenched power. Religious idealism can only moderate the brutal and antisocial elements of the powerful; it can never eliminate them. This is why, according to Niebuhr, the simple moralistic message, "love thy neighbor," of liberal Protestantism, is heard cynically by exploited social groups. Therefore, Niebuhr did not hesitate to urge the dispossessed to take matters into their own hands. Whether they are Indians in Asia or blacks in the United States, the oppressed "have a higher moral right to challenge their oppressors than these have to maintain their rule by force."[31] Morality is always on the side of the exploited social groups; hence, the use of power is justified in the struggle to achieve social justice.

Further light can be shed on Niebuhr's views on power by an examination of his interpretation of the meaning and relationship between love and justice. The relationship between love and justice was the primary emphasis in Niebuhr's thought, and the relationship was conceived not in dualistic but in dialectical terms. Niebuhr explained:

> The positive relation of principles of justice to the ideal of brotherhood makes an indeterminate approximation of love in the realm of justice possible. The negative relation means that all historic conceptions of justice will embody some elements which contradict the law of love.[32]

As this statement indicates, for Niebuhr love and justice should be distinguished, but they should never be separated. Love is the fulfillment of justice in the sense that love serves to expand the potential of justice; love is the negation of justice in that love always transcends justice and sits in judgment upon every historical actualization of justice.

In Niebuhr's thought, the demands of the Christian ethic as stated by Jesus in the Sermon on the Mount and elsewhere are absolute and unconditional. Christians should love their neighbors in the way that God has loved them — disinterestedly, unqualifiedly, and without consideration of the worth of the object. Christians are presented with an ethic, declared Niebuhr, that they cannot disavow because it judges their prudential decisions, but which they cannot perfectly achieve because of egoism and vested interests. This is the source of Niebuhr's description of the Christian ethic as an "impossible possibility." But one should not infer from this that he considered the ethic of love to be irrelevant to historical life. He hastened to speak of "the relevance of an impossible ethical ideal."[33] This was a logical step because Niebuhr's intention was not to denigrate the ethic of love; to the contrary, he was searching for an adequate strategy to implement it, given the fact of human egoism and the complexity of social evil. There is, in his view, a profound relevance of the ethic of love for both the personal and the social dimensions of life because, although never fully achieved in history, it provides "an absolute standard by which to judge both personal and social righteousness."[34] In interpersonal and small group relations (e.g., family), it is often possible to achieve a high degree of unselfish love. In these relations it is easier, relatively speaking, to meet the needs of the neighbor without weighing and measuring them against those of the self.

As Niebuhr grappled with the problem of the relevance of the Christian ethic, he came to the conclusion that its relevance to social relations was quite different from its relevance to interpersonal and small group relations. As one enters multi-personal and group relations wherein decisions must be made between competing neighbor claims, the love ideal is necessarily refracted. That is, in the complex human relations of society, the ethical goal is not love but justice. Justice is the highest approximation of love that finite humans can achieve in social institutions and social structures. But love is always related to justice because it is the motive behind all attempts to achieve justice; furthermore, love is the norm by which all systems of justice should be evaluated. When measured by the norm of love, every system of justice is imperfect, and every social program is a compromise. Thus the Christian is constantly forced to choose between alternative social programs on the basis of how closely they approximate the norm of love.

Niebuhr erupted in violent protest against the failure of liberal Protestantism to understand the dialectical relation between love and justice, its tendency to equate the two and thereby to succumb to the sentimentality of proposing love as the cure for every social problem. Niebuhr considered it utopian, given the depth of humanity's collective egoism, to expect races, classes, and nations to live by the law of love. He denounced as simple moralism the tendency of liberal Christians to substitute love for justice on the grounds that it led to the acceptance of less than the maximum justice that might be possible in any given context.

Having thus exposed the simple moralism of liberal Protestantism, Niebuhr continued on to lay siege to liberalism's juxtaposition of love and power. He traced the social ineffectiveness of the church to its failure to devise an adequate strategy to deal with groups with entrenched power. The children of light often forget, unfortunately, that all systems of justice have been realized by establishing an equilibrium of power within a society. Niebuhr suggested a strategy in his concept of the "balance of power." He appreciated what he called "second-rate goodness" and "the intolerable harmonies of life," though he readily conceded that the system of justice achieved by a balance of power is different from and inferior to love. However, this does not mean that a balance of power excludes love. "In fact," he explained, "without love the frictions and tensions of a balance of power would become intolerable. But without the balance of power even the most loving relations may degenerate into unjust relations. . . ."[35] In short, the use of power and coercion may be necessary to achieve social justice. Love and power should not be juxtaposed, just as love and justice should not be separated. Power may be an instrument of justice, and justice is an instrument of love.

By the time King wrote *Where Do We Go from Here: Chaos or Community?* in 1967, he had arrived at a position on the relationship between power, justice, and love which was similar to that of Reinhold Niebuhr. Although there were differences in emphasis and mode of expression at some points, the substance was

quite similar. That King understood and agreed with the necessity of power, as Niebuhr had stated it, is clear beyond question.
This is evident in his suggestion that the Southern Christian
Leadership Conference should give top priority to the study of
"the levers of power" that blacks should understand in order to
achieve their goals, and that they should assign the development
of programs to a secondary position. King was convinced that it
would be possible to locate "the levers of power" because, though
often perceived with difficulty, they are usually economic in origin. This statement reflects the Marxist analysis of Niebuhr in
Moral Man and Immoral Society. King's experiences with Southern culture and Southern Christians had taught him a painful
truth: "In the South," he wrote, "businessmen act much more
quickly from economic considerations than do churchmen from
moral considerations."[36]

The ideological (i.e., economic) determination of morality was
brought home to King in a dramatic way during the Birmingham
campaign. In their struggle for equal public accommodations,
blacks in Birmingham had sought help from United States Steel,
a powerful, northern-based industry, which ostensibly had little
to lose from involvement in the racial crisis in an Alabama city.
After some time, however, Roger Blough, Chairman of the Board
of United States Steel, replied that "it would be improper for the
corporation to seek to influence community policies in race relations." If the Birmingham City Council, King responded, were to
enact laws that would adversely affect the economic conditions
of United States Steel, Roger Blough's reply would surely have
been different.[37]

As a result of such experiences and many others, King recognized the validity of the Niebuhrian argument about the direct
relationship between privilege and power. As this relationship
crystallized in his mind, he began to feel that the achievement
of an integrated society would be difficult to achieve because
"privileged groups, historically, have not volunteered to give up
privileges."[38] The nonrational character of a privileged group's
defiance in the presence of a threat to its power is evidenced

in the bitterness and hostility it expresses even when the underprivileged strive for freedom and justice through love and nonviolence. Thus, the more King learned about economic and political power, the more he began to raise questions about the efficacy of moral persuasion as a strategy of social change. At one time (1961) he could say that President Kennedy was making "a significant contribution toward the elimination of racial discrimination" by the use of "moral persuasion."[39] But in *Where Do We Go from Here: Chaos or Community?* King concluded that it was utopian to believe "that ethical appeals and persuasion alone will bring about justice. This does not mean that ethical appeals must not be made. It simply means that those appeals must be undergirded by some form of constructive *coercive* power."[40]

One of the difficult lessons King learned in the civil rights struggle was that oppressed people "cannot depend upon American institutions to function without pressure."[41] As he matured, he discovered that one has to deal directly with the structures of society that perpetuate injustice and either modify or eliminate them. Changes in structures usually occur only as a result of the exercise of countervailing power by the oppressed. An equilibrium of power must be established between the various social groups of a society in order for all groups to receive their just share of the products of society. It is significant that King came to this conclusion about the same time that he began to criticize Booker T. Washington, the moderate, and to make favorable comments about W. E. B. Du Bois, the radical. "Washington's error," King observed, "was that he underestimated the structures of evil; as a consequence his philosophy of pressureless persuasion only served as a springboard for racist Southerners to dive into deeper and more ruthless oppression of the Negro."[42] By way of contrast, Du Bois was concerned with the use of coercive power to relieve oppression and to achieve liberation and social justice for all black people.

Although King did not systematically delineate his understanding of the relationship between justice and love, it is one of the main themes of his writings. King's devastating criticism of the white liberal's sentimentality on this subject reflects Niebuhr's own analytical skill. King writes with feeling:

> It is not enough to say "We love Negroes, we have many Negro friends." They [i.e., white liberals] must demand justice for Negroes. Love that does not satisfy justice is no love at all. It is merely a sentimental affection, little more than what one would have for a pet. Love at its best is justice concretized.[43]

Since King's interpretation of love has already been considered in chapter 3, only his interpretation of justice and the relationship between love, power, and justice need to be considered here.

The meaning of justice in King's thought follows closely the natural law tradition of Western thought, though his categories of expression were drawn largely from personalism and philosophical idealism. This is not surprising if the influence of Paul Ramsey, already considered in chapter 3, is taken seriously. Ramsey had argued in *Basic Christian Ethics* (chapter 9) that Christian love is always in search of a social policy and that in the attempt to move from love to decisions about alternative social policies Christian ethicists should utilize the concept of the "natural rights" of humans as it had been expressed in philosophical idealism. In the theistic version of the natural law tradition and the tradition of philosophical idealism, there had always been a close relationship between "the laws of nature" and "the laws of God." When King spoke of the moral law of the cosmos which people ignore at their peril, he had in mind the combination of these traditions. Hence, he argued, as already noted, that the goals of the civil rights movement were not only legally and constitutionally right, but they were right also because they were in conformity with the laws of God.

According to King, therefore, justice has a dual meaning: (1) God's justice and righteousness, the ultimate referent; (2) the laws of society, the penultimate referent. In other words, the laws of the state should reflect the will of God or the moral law of the cosmos, the ultimate source and ground of justice among humanity. In one of the classical theistic formulations of this tradition, Thomism, the ultimate referent had been called eternal/natural law and the penultimate referent human/positive law. In the modern version of this approach to justice, justice has come to mean those inalienable rights human beings are "due" because of the sacredness and inherent worth of human personality. The "right ordering" among persons, established and perpetuated by human law, should guarantee to all unqualified freedom, justice, and equality.

In the history of the United States, the rights of humanity have been understood largely in political and civil terms. These rights have found definitive formulation in the Declaration of Independence and the Bill of Rights of the Constitution, the two documents quoted by King more often than any others except the Bible. In these documents, guarantees are provided for freedom of religion, press, assembly, protection against deprivation of life, liberty, and property without due process of law, trial by jury, etc. During recent decades social and economic rights — free access to public accommodations and transportation, the right to equality in education, employment, housing, health, etc. — have been added to political and civil rights. King had all these human rights in mind when he spoke about justice. Such rights constitute "man's due," according to King, and there is nothing abstract about justice so defined: "It is as concrete as having a good job, a good education, a decent house and a share of power."[44]

In his attempt to state more clearly the meaning of justice, King made a distinction between desegregation and integration that throws much light upon what he meant by those terms and also provides a central clue as to how he conceived the relationship between love, justice, and law. In a little-known but pivotal article, "The Ethical Demands of Integration," King wrote:

> The word *segregation* represents a system that is prohibitive; it denies the Negro equal access to schools, parks, restaurants, libraries and the like. *Desegregation* is eliminative and negative, for

it simply removes these legal and social prohibitions. *Integration* is creative, and is therefore more profound and far-reaching than desegregation. Integration is the positive acceptance of desegregation and the welcomed participation of Negroes into the total range of human activities.[45]

As this quotation indicates, King saw society moving from segregation to desegregation to integration. Desegregation removes the legal and social prohibitions against freedom and equality, but it is essentially negative. By way of contrast, integration is the ultimate goal of society, the actualization of genuine intergroup and interpersonal relations; it is virtually synonymous with the "community of love" that will be produced by adherence to the will of God and the moral law of the cosmos. The important thing to note here is that King associated justice with the middle ground of desegregation. Desegregation is the goal of justice; integration is the goal of love. Love is the goal; justice is the means. Justice involves those aspects of social relations that can be achieved by law. In a word, law is an instrument of justice, and justice is an instrument of love.

Concerning the relationship between love and law, King took a realistic position similar to that of Reinhold Niebuhr. To those who maintained that "morality may not be legislated," King responded affirmatively, but he was quick to counter that "behavior can be regulated." "It may be true," he explained, "that the law can't make a man love me but it can keep him from lynching me...."[46] To understand this distinction is to find the clue to why King would not take sides completely with either those who advocated education or those who advanced legislation as the solution to the racial crisis. He chose to be dialectical again — both education and legislation are needed. Education, along with religion, will help to change the attitudes and hearts of people while legislation will help to control behavior. "Judicial decrees," King wrote in language strikingly similar to Niebuhr, "may not change the heart, but they can restrain the heartless."[47]

King felt that it is immoral to compel a person to endure injustice while waiting for another's heart to change. He knew that
it is impossible to change a person's attitudes through legislation; laws are not intended to do that. But he did not consider
this fact to be a justification for quietism or political inaction.
Although laws cannot change attitudes, they can control the behavior that results from attitudes. The provision for justice by
the state through laws does not contradict the ethic of love; it
is rather an indispensable means to enhance the welfare of society as a whole and thus, indirectly, the welfare of the individual.
The structural framework of society, including laws, performs the
work of love insofar as the framework fosters justice for all. This
explains the emphasis (far too great, claim many of his critics)
King placed upon laws and the rigorous enforcement of them by
the federal government.

The consideration of King's views on love, justice, and law
brings one to the place where further insight can be gained
about the importance of power in King's thought. King came
reluctantly to the conclusion that there would be no painless
transition from the old order of injustice to a new order of justice because the effort to root out entrenched power is always
fraught with tension and conflict. An oppressed group, like blacks
in the United States, cannot achieve its rights without confrontation and constant pressure upon the social groups wherein
power is concentrated. King sadly acknowledged that a black
person

> cannot achieve emancipation by passively waiting for the white
> race voluntarily to grant it to him. The Negro has not gained a
> single right in America without persistent pressure and agitation.
> However lamentable it may seem, the Negro is now convinced
> that white America will never admit him to equal rights unless it
> is coerced into doing it.[48]

This was King's way of stating that justice and power are
integrally related.

King's most articulate statement of the relationship between
love, power, and justice was made in response to the shift in

emphasis in the civil rights movement signaled by the advent of "Black Power" (1966) as expressed primarily by Stokely Carmichael. King agonized over the Black Power movement because, although he understood that it had arisen as a result of the lack of progress in the achievement of genuine gains for blacks, he had serious reservations about its connotations (i.e., separatism) and implications (i.e., violence). The statement King produced in response to the increasing militancy of some segments of the civil rights movement is a distillation of much of his mature ethical thought. Note especially the call for a "balance of power" and the foolishness of setting love over against power, both Niebuhrian themes already mentioned earlier. King wrote:

> Power, properly understood, is the ability to achieve purpose. It is the strength required to bring about social, political or economic changes. In this sense power is not only desirable but necessary in order to implement the demands of love and justice. One of the greatest problems of history is that the concepts of love and power are usually contrasted as polar opposites. Love is identified with a resignation of power and power with a denial of love.... What is needed is a realization that power without love is reckless and abusive and that love without power is sentimental and anemic. Power at its best is love implementing the demands of justice. Justice at its best is love correcting everything that stands against love.[49]

As King's thought matured, he accepted the importance of power in the struggle for social justice. He acknowledged that the main road of escape from oppression by blacks would be an equitable sharing of political and economic power between blacks and whites, and he was aware that the effort to achieve this would lead to social conflict in which "the power structure" would be pitted against the oppressed. It is probably true, given King's debt to liberalism and the social gospel, that King reluctantly faced that reality.

Martin Luther King did not repudiate Reinhold Niebuhr or turn Niebuhrianism "upside down," as James Sellers alleges.[50] To the contrary, King agreed with Niebuhr that love is the ultimate norm of the Christian ethic, that love transcends justice and sits in judgment upon all finite systems of justice. Further, all achievements of justice in human society fall short of love, and love reaches beyond justice to raise all expressions of justice to new heights. Nevertheless, love should not be used as a substitute for justice because human beings cannot be forced to live by the law of love. Hence, justice is also necessary; however, structures of justice should not be viewed as "eternal norms" but rather as attempts "to strike a balance between the final moral possibilities of life and the immediate and given realities."[51] To limit love to justice, on the one hand, is to put love in a straitjacket so that it becomes less than *agape*. When love is divorced from justice, on the other hand, love often becomes pious sentimentality so that the maximum justice possible in any given situation is not achieved.

NONVIOLENCE AND PACIFISM

When King wrote that he was "confused" by his initial study of Niebuhr, he was referring primarily to Niebuhr's critique of nonviolence and pacifism. It is helpful to remember that King's encounter with Niebuhr occurred shortly after his study of Gandhi, in whose thought and activity King claimed to have found the proper method to fight against social injustice, and that Niebuhr's critique of nonviolence in *Moral Man and Immoral Society* had been focused upon Gandhi. It is also necessary to point out that absolute pacifism (i.e., nonresistance) and nonviolence (i.e., nonviolent direct action) were not synonymous for either Niebuhr or King. Niebuhr denounced absolute pacifism on the grounds that it was utterly unrealistic. On the other hand, he defended nonviolence as an effective pragmatic strategy for members of an oppressed group in their struggle for social justice. Whereas King had a great deal of difficulty with Niebuhr's critique of Gandhian nonviolence, Niebuhr's critique of absolute pacifism had a positive and enduring influence upon his thought.

Nonviolence and Nonresistance

In order to understand Niebuhr's views on nonresistance and nonviolence, it is necessary to comprehend the way he interpreted the Christian ethic. For Niebuhr the norm of the Christian ethic is the law of love (*agape*), expressed supremely in the cross of Jesus Christ and Jesus' life and teachings. He agreed with Ernst Troeltsch that Jesus' ethic is best described as "an ethic of 'love universalism and love perfectionism.'"[52] Jesus intended that all his teachings, such as "turn the other cheek," "love your enemies," etc., should be taken literally. Accordingly, Niebuhr described the ethic of Jesus in unconditional and unequivocal terms. The Christian ethic is a radical ethic; it demands the sacrifice of the self for the neighbor or a noble cause. Christians should love the neighbor, including the enemy-neighbor, the way God loves human beings, disinterestedly, absolutely, and with no thought about the worth of the object.

Having begun with the definition of the Christian ethic as a "love perfectionism," Niebuhr concluded that nonresistance (i.e., passive resistance) is the only truly Christian response to provocation of any kind. The only way to live strictly by "the way of the cross" is to withdraw from the ego rivalries and competitive struggles of history. Insofar as one enters the social, political, and economic conflicts generated by historical existence, one becomes involved inevitably in the use of either psychological or physical coercion — both explicitly prohibited by the ethic of Jesus. There is no basis in the New Testament, according to Niebuhr, for the argument of those liberals who equate the ethic of Jesus with nonviolent resistance. Niebuhr regarded the linkage of nonviolent resistance with the ethic of Jesus as a dilution of the absolute ethic of Jesus. Further, such a linkage leads to confusion because it presupposes a distinction between nonviolent and violent coercion that cannot be justified. (Niebuhr considered nonviolence to be a form of psychological coercion.)

The point is that Niebuhr wished to draw the distinction between nonresistance and nonviolent resistance as sharply as possible because he believed that they had often been confused. He went on to cite Mahatma Gandhi, whom he recognized as "the greatest modern exponent of non-violence" and the last person King would expect, as the major culprit in the perpetration of this confusion. Niebuhr argued that Gandhi confused the distinction between nonresistance and nonviolent resistance because of the terminology Gandhi used to express his position. Niebuhr reasoned that since Gandhi identified "soul-force" with the spiritual and "body-force" with the physical, he gave the impression that nonviolence is passive resistance, not active resistance.[53] It is true that Niebuhr's quarrel with Gandhi seemed to go deeper than semantics since Niebuhr referred to nonviolence as "a passive and negative form of resistance."[54] But Niebuhr's choice of words here was unfortunate because the context indicates that he was not accusing Gandhi of equating nonviolent resistance with nonresistance; rather, Niebuhr was comparing nonviolent resistance with violent resistance. At any rate, such phrases apparently confused King and led him to charge Niebuhr with misrepresenting Gandhi at this crucial point.

Insofar as King's reaction to Niebuhr's critique of Gandhi was based on King's belief that Niebuhr had inaccurately described Gandhi as an advocate of nonresistance, King's confusion and his reply to Niebuhr are understandable; in fact, his reply is right on target. King responded to Niebuhr that Gandhi had advocated nonviolent resistance not nonresistance, and that nonviolence is an active not a passive form of resistance. In King's words, nonviolence "is not unrealistic submission to evil power, as Niebuhr contends. It is rather a courageous confrontation of evil by the power of love, in the faith that it is better to be the recipient of violence than the inflicter of it. . . . "[55] According to King, nonviolence is an active form of resistance which uses the method of love instead of hate.

As already indicated in chapter 3, King understood Gandhi's position and stated it correctly. However, it seems that King misunderstood what Niebuhr had attempted to do in his critique of Gandhi. A close scrutiny of Niebuhr's assessment of Gandhi clearly shows that Niebuhr did not accuse Gandhi of advocating nonresistance or passive resistance. Niebuhr's point was that although Gandhi advocated nonviolent resistance in the form of strikes, boycotts, and civil disobedience, Gandhi persisted in using terminology that connoted nonresistance. The distinction between nonresistance and nonviolent resistance is quite clear in Niebuhr's thought. Niebuhr's definition of the meaning of nonviolence and his description of its characteristics are in complete harmony with the summary of Gandhi's and King's thought as stated in chapter 3.[56] (Niebuhr's footnotes in *Moral Man and Immoral Society* and *The Nature and Destiny of Man* indicate that he used many of the same sources King would use later.) Niebuhr commended Gandhi for the use of nonviolence against the British in India, and he lauded King for adopting nonviolence as the strategy of the civil rights movement in the United States. There were, to be sure, fundamental differences between Gandhi and Niebuhr which led Niebuhr to criticize Gandhi at crucial points, but these criticisms did not stem from Gandhi's failure to distinguish between nonviolent resistance and nonresistance.[57]

The value that Niebuhr assigned to nonviolent resistance shines forth like a beacon in the closing pages of *Moral Man and Immoral Society,* wherein he suggested that the black minority in the United States would profit significantly from the use of nonviolence. Gandhi's success in India convinced Niebuhr that "non-violence is a particularly strategic instrument for an oppressed group which is hopelessly in the minority and has no possibility of developing sufficient power to set against its oppressors."[58] In his elaboration of this thesis, Niebuhr penned in 1932 one of the most prophetic passages of the twentieth century, and it came to fruition a quarter of a century later in the activity of Martin Luther King. Niebuhr wrote:

> The emancipation of the Negro race in America probably waits upon the adequate development of this kind of social and political strategy [i.e., nonviolent direct action]. It is hopeless for the Negro to expect complete emancipation from the menial social and economic position into which the white man has forced

him, merely by trusting in the moral sense of the white race. It is equally hopeless to attempt emancipation through violent rebellion....

...However large the number of individual white men who do and who will identify themselves completely with the Negro cause, the white race in America will not admit the Negro to equal rights if it is not forced to do so. Upon that point one may speak with a dogmatism which all history justifies.

On the other hand, any effort at violent revolution on the part of the Negro will accentuate the animosities and prejudices of his oppressors. Since they outnumber him hopelessly, any appeal to arms must inevitably result in a terrible social catastrophe. Social ignorance and economic interest are arrayed against him....

The technique of non-violence will not eliminate all these perils. But it will reduce them. It will, if persisted in with the same patience and discipline attained by Mr. Gandhi and his followers, achieve a degree of justice which neither pure moral suasion nor violence could gain.[59]

Martin Luther King must have read this passage again and again; moreover, the passage indicates why *Moral Man and Immoral Society* was one of King's favorite books.

Absolute Pacifism and "Realistic" Pacifism

Reinhold Niebuhr's critique of "absolute" pacifism has become the classical argument for most nonpacifists. Niebuhr, himself, had been a pacifist during the post-World War I era. However, the growing international crisis in the late twenties and early thirties, accentuated by the rise of Adolf Hitler in Germany, led Niebuhr to reexamine and finally to disavow his pacifist convictions. It is important to point out that the kind of pacifism Niebuhr denounced was the "absolute" type (i.e., war should never be an instrument of national policy under any conditions). While Niebuhr conceded, as stated previously, that nonviolence could be an effective pragmatic strategy for oppressed minorities, he took an entirely different attitude toward absolute pacifism, reasoning that in international relations pacifism is usually futile and self-defeating.[60]

One important element of Niebuhr's argument against absolute pacifism included the belief that pacifists, who practice passive resistance (i.e., do nothing), contribute to the triumph of tyranny because tyranny never destroys itself; to the contrary, it always continues to grow unless it is resisted. In order to resist tyranny, overt conflict is usually necessary. Niebuhr's argument assumed that anarchy is always preferable to tyranny because if the goal of transitory anarchy is justice with peace, then anarchy may provide the context for the development of creative alternatives. Herein lies Niebuhr's reason for referring to the violent conflict of war as a "lesser evil" and a "negative good." He was fearful that an absolute disavowal of overt conflict, either domestic or international, would lead to an abandonment of the attempt to struggle for social justice.

Niebuhr's argument against absolute pacifism was based upon his interpretation of human nature. Pacifists, he contended, do not understand human nature well enough to perceive the perennial contradiction between the law of love and the sin of humanity. He saw absolute pacifists as excellent examples of the ethic of "love perfectionism" because they considered the law of love to be a simple historical possibility. This position assumed, according to Niebuhr, that human nature is essentially good and rational, and that with time, education, patience, and long-suffering, the demonic persons and structures of society responsible for injustice will eventually crumble. Unfortunately, Niebuhr countered, pacifists are mistaken in their belief that love will prevail if only good people are more resolute because the egoistic impulse of human nature usually prevents the actualization of love in personal and group relations. The selfishness of human beings cannot be controlled simply by appealing to their conscience. Human beings are unable to transcend the complexities and ambiguities of history and the claims and counterclaims of vested interests. Appeals to goodwill and conscience are ultimately of no avail unless individuals recognize their sin and are justified by the grace of God.

In spite of his withering attack upon absolute pacifism,

Niebuhr went on to point out two significant contributions pacifism can make to society. In the first place, the pacifist, provided
he or she is aware of the degree to which he or she is "a parasite
on the sins of his fellowmen," provides "a valuable reminder to
the Christian community of the fact that the Kingdom of God
has come and that its law is the law of life, even though men
cannot maintain themselves in the world of sin by obedience
to it."[61] Therefore, the church is wise to protect its pacifists.
They bear a relevant witness to the love (*agape*) that is unattain-
able in history and yet that love must be the object of human
endeavor — a love which judges and ultimately heals us.

In the second place, Niebuhr defended what he called a "pragmatic" pacifism. This type of pacifism does not use the law of
love as its model; rather, it accepts the world "as it is," a world
characterized by struggles for power and the need to restrain the
violent competition of selfish interests. According to Niebuhr,
the concern of pragmatic pacifism lies

> ...in mitigating the struggle between contending forces, by in-
> sinuating the greatest possible degree of social imagination and
> intelligence into it and by providing the best possible means of ar-
> bitration so that violent conflict may be avoided. Such a pacifism
> is a necessary influence in every society because social violence is
> a great evil and ought to be avoided if at all possible.[62]

Reinhold Niebuhr's probing analysis of the complexity of
human relationships, his exposition of the need for countervailing power, and his exposure of self-righteousness even in the most
saintly left an indelible mark upon King's view of absolute pacifism. He shared Niebuhr's observation that many pacifists fail
to see the duplicity and ambiguity in all human acts, and their
"unwarranted optimism concerning man" comes perilously close
to self-righteousness. After studying Niebuhr, King described his
position as "realistic pacifism," and his explanation sounds very
much like Niebuhr's "pragmatic pacifism." "I came to see," King
wrote, "the pacifist position not as sinless but as the lesser evil in
the circumstances. I felt...that the pacifist would have a greater
appeal if he did not claim to be free from the moral dilemmas

that the Christian nonpacifist confronts."[63] Niebuhr's point that absolute pacifists suffer from moral illusions was duly noted and remembered by King. It appears that King saw a moral ambiguity in the absolute pacifist position that only a few of its adherents would grant.[64]

That King was a "realistic" not a "doctrinaire" pacifist is illustrated best perhaps in his positive attitude toward the use of force in society under certain circumstances. When the National Guard, army troops, and federal marshals were utilized to assure James Meredith's admission to the University of Mississippi, King regretted the need for force, but he did not hesitate to state that it was "necessary and justifiable." "Whereas I abhor the use of arms and the thought of war," King responded, "I do believe in the intelligent use of police power.... Mississippi's breakdown of law and order demanded the utilization of a police action to quell the disorder and enforce the law of the land."[65]

Reinhold Niebuhr commended King's realistic pacifism and his interpretation of nonviolence. He rejoiced over King's practicality, and he was jubilant about the outcome of the Montgomery bus boycott. D. B. Robertson quotes Niebuhr as saying that "Martin Luther King's position is right" and that he is "the most creative Protestant, white or black."[66]

In the foreword to a pamphlet on the Vietnam war, Niebuhr refers to King as "one of the great religious leaders of our time."[67] Niebuhr defended King's use of nonviolent resistance against those who had confused it with the absolute pacifism that they rejected. However, it is not surprising, given Niebuhr's interpretation of the Christian ethic, that he criticized King for referring to the Montgomery boycott as "the way of love." "Love," Niebuhr responded, "is a motive and not a method." But Niebuhr hastened to explain:

> Those of us who are non-pacifists will be quick to admit that whenever pacifism is not preoccupied with moral scruples and guiltlessness and personal perfection; whenever it does not occupy itself with the problem of contracting out of responsibilities

of justice in the name of personal perfection, whenever it seeks for justice, it becomes impressive.[68]

There is no doubt that Niebuhr believed King's version of pacifism and his use of nonviolence fulfilled those requirements and that his success in Montgomery had been impressive.

Reinhold Niebuhr did not change his mind about King after the developments in the civil rights movement subsequent to Montgomery. Niebuhr continued to hold that "King's conception of nonviolent resistance to evil is a real contribution to our civil, moral and political life."[69] A letter written to one of the authors in September 1969 undoubtedly contains Niebuhr's final remarks on King:

> ...my enthusiasm for Dr. King's nonviolence despite my anti-pacifism was due to my distinction between a pacifism designed to prove our purity and a pacifism designed to establish justice. I thought that Dr. King leading a ten percent Negro minority was a good combination of idealism and pragmatic realism.[70]

Niebuhr's insight is right on target; it properly emphasizes the realistic, pragmatic dimension of King's version of nonviolence and nonviolent direct action.

CHAPTER FIVE

Personalism

MARTIN LUTHER KING'S decision to pursue graduate studies for the Doctor of Philosophy degree in theology and philosophy at the School of Theology of Boston University was no accident. Across the years many black students had attended Boston University, and they had found a congenial atmosphere in which to study. A more important attraction for King was the presence of Edgar Sheffield Brightman whose philosophy of personalism King had studied at Crozer Seminary with George W. Davis. The personalism of Brightman was by far the single most important philosophical influence upon Davis's theology. Brightman's book A *Philosophy of Religion* was the major text in Davis's philosophy of religion courses. In addition, Brightman was well known and highly respected by the Crozer faculty as a whole. Morton Scott Enslin, editor of *The Crozer Quarterly*, introduced him to the *Quarterly's* readers as "a frequent and ever-welcome contributor."[1]

Boston University had been associated with the personalist school of philosophy for three-quarters of a century prior to King's application to study there. Borden Parker Bowne, the first and one of the best-known American personalists, had been appointed professor of philosophy at Boston University in 1876. Between that time and the present, Boston University has been well known for such outstanding personalist scholars as Brightman and Peter Bertocci (a student of Brightman's), Albert C. Knudson (a student of Bowne's) and L. Harold DeWolf in theology, and Walter G. Muelder in social ethics. King was greatly indebted to all of these scholars. He said that Brightman "contributed most to the shaping of his character."[2] DeWolf was his major professor and adviser for his dissertation.

King took a total of fifteen courses at Boston University for his doctoral studies, ten of them in biblical and systematic theology and philosophy of religion with Brightman and DeWolf. King's graduate courses at Boston University expanded and deepened his knowledge of personalism that had been covered previously in an introductory fashion at Crozer Seminary.* One has only to look at King's innumerable references to the "sacredness of human personality," "the legacy of dignity and worth" to which every person is heir, and his constant reference to "the moral law of the cosmos" that unfolds inevitably within history to see the profound influence of personalism.

The impact of Brightman and DeWolf, personally and intellectually, upon King's thought was recorded by him in these words:

> Both men greatly stimulated my thinking. It was mainly under these teachers that I studied personalistic philosophy — the theory that the clue to the meaning of ultimate reality is found in personality. This personal idealism remains today my basic philosophical position. Personalism's insistence that only personality — finite and infinite — is ultimately real strengthened me in two convictions; it gave me metaphysical and philosophical grounding for the idea of a personal God, and it gave me a metaphysical basis for the dignity and worth of all human personality.[3]

With the exception of this quotation, King makes no other specific references to personalism per se. However, in many places throughout his writings, in short phrases as well as discussions of various subjects, the influence of the theistic idealism of personalism is unmistakably present.

---

*The authors do not claim that personalism was the only subject that was deepened and broadened by King's studies at Boston, but that this subject seems to have been the most important. It is quite clear, for example, that King continued to study Reinhold Niebuhr and that he made his first intensive study of Hegel at Boston University. (See term papers on Niebuhr and Hegel in the Boston Collection.)

PERSONALISM, IDEALISM, AND THEISM

In one form or another, all of the exponents of personalism (Bowne, Brightman, Knudson, etc.) espoused a metaphysical system in which personality was the organizing principle or central category. "The metaphysics of personalism," Knudson said, "may be summed up in the statement that personality is the key to reality."[4] "In the broadest sense," Brightman wrote, "personalism is the belief that conscious personality is both the supreme value and the supreme reality in the universe."[5] Knudson and Brightman considered personality to be fundamental to all knowledge and essential to an understanding of all reality. In short, the basic fact of existence is not abstract thought or a thought process, but a person, a self, or a thinker.

But personalists do not stop with the assertion that personality is the key to the meaning of reality. Personalists also affirm that personality has ontological status; it is the clue to ultimate reality. They contend that not only is personality the central category of reality but also that the process which produces and sustains personality is also personal. This means, metaphysically speaking, that personality is the only adequate category available to describe God, the Supreme Cause of the universe and the only perfect personality. All finite personalities are faint copies of the Supreme Personality. According to this approach, the universe is a society of persons, and the central and most creative person is God. All reality participates in ultimate reality (i.e., God) because the universe is an organic whole. Human beings, however, have a special dignity and worth among created things. Such an ontology obviously has a place for both religious and ethical concerns. This potential was perceived by King, and he responded enthusiastically to such an approach.

In his explication of the meaning of personalism, Brightman made a distinction between "self" and "person." "A self," he explained, "is any conscious process; a person is a self that can experience values and judge itself by rational norms."[6] "Person" is a more inclusive concept than "self" because the former possesses attributes which the latter does not. By this distinction personalists attempted to highlight the priority of the human and the personal over the impersonal and irrational aspects of the processes of nature. Knudson argued, for example, that a person is a self that has attained some degree of intellectual and moral development. Neither a child nor a slave is a person in the true sense of the word, because personhood implies freedom and responsibility. This is one of the reasons that King indicted segregation and discrimination as depersonalizing and dehumanizing.

Further light may be shed upon the meaning of personalism if it is kept in mind that many of personalism's themes reflect the tradition of idealism in Western philosophy. Knudson stated categorically: "thoroughgoing personalism is idealistic."[7] The themes of idealism pervade the literature of personalist philosophers and theologians. According to idealism, the body is conceived as a container of the mind or spirit. But the personalists who influenced King did not deny the existence of the physical world as "subjective" idealists had done. The personalists who influenced King drew upon the tradition of "objective" idealism — the version of idealism that affirmed the existence of the world independently of human perception of it. The personal character of the cosmos is discovered by human beings, not simply projected from their minds. The universe is viewed as an intelligible order because its structures express rational coherence and value.

Although the personalists who influenced King were objective idealists, they still maintained that the most important aspects of reality are *invisible* and *nonsensible*. Yet there is a vital relationship between the visible and the invisible. Reality has a continuity and a coherence that come together in personality which unites all of the varied experiences of time and space. Personality is a manifestation of ultimate reality, and the locus of ultimate reality is a "Supreme Personality," a form of superior intelligence apart from which nothing has existence or meaning. All visible and sensible life is a manifestation of the invisible, creative nature of the Supreme Person.

As a dedicated apologist for the reality of the nonsensible, Brightman strongly defended the invisibility of the personal world. The body can be seen, but not personality. Sense experiences do not give us a direct perception of the experience in another person's mind. Brightman even questioned whether sense experience alone can provide adequate knowledge of the body. Beginning with this assumption, he criticized those schools of thought like behaviorism, naturalism, and logical positivism, which attempt to restrict meaning and knowledge to the sensible world (i.e., if something cannot be verified in sense experience, it is untrue). "Imagine what human culture would be," he said, "if this restriction were taken seriously, and all references to ideals, purposes, truth, and consciousness were actually supposed to be meaningless!"[8] He contended that ideals and values could not possibly be accounted for on the basis of the assumptions of empiricism and positivism. Systems of thought that restrict reality to the visible and sensible ignore "the most essential characteristic of all experience, namely, that it is personal consciousness."[9] Brightman considered his position to be more empirical and more scientific than materialism or naturalism because it was more inclusive. "Personalism," Brightman concluded, "is a philosophy whose interpreters seek for a unity that includes all the facts — the facts of value and personality as well as the facts of the sense order."[10]

On the basis of such beliefs, Brightman attacked what he called "the realistic creed" of "every man for himself." Although there is conflict and selfishness in human relations, there is also self-sacrifice and love of peace and truth. While he did not deny the positive value of conflict and the constructive results that often issue from it, Brightman argued, using language similar to passages in King's writings, " . . . that beyond all war there is peace, beyond all chaos there is order, beyond all seeming contradictions there is coherent truth. Everything noble in human history grows out of some dim apprehension of this truth."[11]

Martin Luther King was influenced significantly by the themes of idealism in personalism. He said that human beings have

"spiritual experiences that cannot be explained in material-
istic terms," and that "the love and faith" that have made
humankind's greatest cultural achievements possible, such as
the construction of magnificent cathedrals, are never seen. King
often expressed this theme in his sermons:

> As you presently gaze at the pulpit and witness me preaching
> this sermon, you may immediately conclude that you see Mar-
> tin Luther King. But then you are reminded that you see only
> my body, which in itself can neither reason nor think. You can
> never see the *me* that makes me me, and I can never see the *you*
> that makes you you. That invisible something we call personality
> is beyond our physical gaze. Plato was right when he said that the
> visible is a shadow cast by the invisible.[12]

The personalism of Bowne and Brightman provided a metaphysical base and a philosophical rationale for theism. The
exponents of personalism, as previously indicated, gave personality an ontological status by relating it to a Supreme Personality.
Such an ontology made room for a conception of God — a conception that was more akin to theism than to either deism or
pantheism. For deism God is wholly transcendent; for pantheism God is totally immanent. According to personalism, God is
both transcendent and immanent, both free and personal, both
creative and moral. Personalists used many philosophical terms
to describe ultimate reality, such as World Ground, Supreme
Cause, Supreme Person, Supreme Being — all of them were in-
terchangeable with the term "God" in Christian theology. Many
personalist philosophers had a deeply personal religious faith,
and their strictly theological formulations were strikingly similar to those of evangelical liberalism. This was especially true
of Edgar Sheffield Brightman. It is highly likely that one of the
major tenets of King's conception of nonviolence, "the redemptive value of unmerited suffering," was indebted to Brightman in
whose thought "the spiritual value of sacrifice and suffering" was
one of the essentials of Christian theology.[13]

In an age when theology was besieged by empiricism and

science, many theologians found in personalism a metaphysical foundation for theology that conserved what they considered to be the basic tenets of historic Christianity. Knudson, for example, considered the emphasis of personalism upon personality, both divine and human, to be the essence of Christianity. Thus he saw personalism as the philosophy that was closer to Christianity than any other. "The magic word 'personality,'" he wrote, "by virtue of the new insight it gives us into the nature of reality and into the conditions of knowledge, binds together historical Christianity and the personalistic philosophy."[14] Hence, personalism is often called Christian idealism. Equally understandable is King's testimony to personalism cited above: it provided him "a metaphysical and philosophical grounding for the idea of a personal God, and...for the dignity and worth of all human personality."[15]

THEMES OF PERSONALISM IN KING'S THOUGHT

Several themes occur and recur in King's writings that are clearly traceable to the influence of personalism. These themes may be treated under the following headings: (1) the inherent worth of personality, (2) the personal God of love and reason, (3) the moral law of the cosmos, and (4) the social nature of human existence.

The Inherent Worth of Personality

Edgar Sheffield Brightman delineated the basic principles of the philosophy of personalism in summary form near the end of *Nature and Values*. One of the major principles is "respect for personality." He explained what he meant by that phrase in terms of three levels of personhood. At one level, it means a healthy self-respect — "never knowingly to violate either my reason or my love."[16] At another level, it means respect for the dignity and worth of other selves. In language reminiscent of Kant, Brightman stated what he called "The Law of the Ideal of Personality": "*All persons ought to judge and guide all of their acts by their ideal conception . . . of what the whole personality ought to become both individually and socially.*"[17] Finally, it connotes respect for God, the Divine Personality. Unlike human beings who may be respected for what they can become, God can be respected for what God is because it is inherent to the Divine nature to respect personality. Every form of life, conscious and unconscious, is a manifestation of the Supreme Person. Since the Supreme Person is the source and conserver of values, all life is inherently valuable.

Brightman elaborated upon the meaning of the inherent worth of personality in his conception of "spiritual liberty." He contended that the entire history of the human race has been a struggle for freedom. His understanding of spiritual liberty went beyond both the familiar conception of freedom of choice and the civil liberties embraced by democratic political theory, though both were accepted by him. According to Brightman, spiritual liberty is the result of "a life in touch with the sources of truth and power. . . . 'The truth shall make you free.'"[18] More specifically, spiritual liberty permits one to become a person in the true sense, to develop one's potential to the fullest extent, to experience one's worth, dignity, and value — in religious terms, to feel that one is loved as a child of God.

There is no single theme more prominent in King's thought than the inherent dignity and worth of personality. He believed that at the heart of the political and religious heritage of Western civilization has been the conviction that "every man is an heir to a legacy of dignity and worth" and that "every human being has etched in his personality the indelible stamp of the Creator."[19] "Our Judeo-Christian tradition," King explained, "refers to this inherent dignity of man in the Biblical term 'the image of God.' 'The image of God' is universally shared in equal portions by all men."[20] It is clear that King equated "image of God" and "infinite metaphysical value," a phrase that appears frequently in the literature of personalism. By virtue of birth every person is a child of God and is related to God as a child to a parent. The worth of a person does not reside in one's degree of intelligence, background, or social status. In King's words, the source of human dignity is not one's "specificity" but one's "fundamentum."[21] By "fundamentum" King meant a person's special relationship to God because of the image of God. Persons have inherent value because they are "a reflection of divinity," not because of an accident of birth or history. "In the final analysis, says the Christian ethic, every man must be respected because God loves him."[22]

With this approach to the source and meaning of human worth, King made a decisive break with orthodox theology, which affirmed that as a consequence of the Fall the image of God in humanity was defaced to such a degree that it could be restored only by the atoning work of Jesus Christ. But King was relatively silent on the atonement as an event that alters significantly the God-person relationship. King interpreted that relationship in terms of the doctrine of Creation instead of the doctrine of the atonement. The explanation for this fact is found, in part, in the interpretation of nature that King found in Brightman: nature is a revelation of God. That is, God is revealed through nature, and nature has a sacramental character — nature is "a sensible sign...of grace and God's good will toward us."[23] Nature is literally God's handiwork and a manifestation of God in action. On the basis of this assumption, plus his belief in the image of God, King stressed the potential goodness of all created things, especially the potentialities of human nature. Even in his darkest moments of despair and doubt, he consistently emphasized the goodness and value of human life instead of its brokenness and depravity.

However, one should not conclude that King ignored the fact of human sin. (As indicated in chapter 4, Reinhold Niebuhr left an indelible mark upon King's thought on this subject.) As a result of sin, the image of God *can* be seriously distorted. This occurs when human beings treat each other so unjustly that their essence is significantly defaced. "Every act of injustice," King observed, "mars and defaces the image of God in man."[24] So long as any person is treated as something less than a person of sacred worth, "the image of God is abused in him and consequently and proportionately lost by those who inflict the abuse."[25] King assumed that human nature is perfectible, and he viewed sin from within the framework of his belief in the inherent worth of human personality.

King's conviction regarding the inherent worth of personality provided the theological and philosophical basis for his attack on segregation. He consistently held that segregation is sinful because it is the fruit of pride and hatred. "The undergirding philosophy of segregation," he stated emphatically, "is diametrically opposed to the undergirding philosophy of our Judeo-Christian heritage, and all the dialectics of the logicians cannot make them lie down together."[26] Further, segregation is immoral because it treats human beings as means to an end rather than as ends in themselves. To treat persons as means to an end is to reduce them to things — objects that are less than human. Since all persons are children of God, they should be "treated as *ends* and never as mere *means*."[27] A person is not a means to an end or a thing; hence, no one should be treated as such. Every person should be treated as a subject of inherent value.

One of King's criticisms of the totalitarianism of communism was based upon his belief in the inherent worth and dignity of personality. Totalitarianism denies human freedom and thus relegates human beings to the status of things rather than elevating them to the status of persons. Such a system would "depersonalize the potential person and...desecrate what he is."[28] Humans were not made for the state, and they should never be used as means to achieve the ends of the state. To the contrary, people are the end for which the state exists. In contrast to totalitarianism, King assumed that democracy at its best is "person-oriented" instead of "thing-oriented." The goal of democracy is a completely integrated society wherein black people will be able to experience "somebodiness" and "self-respect." Furthermore, King's concern to alleviate human need was rooted in "the infinite metaphysical value" of human personality. If people believed that, they would not "be content to see men hungry, to see men victimized with ill-health, when we have the means to help them."[29] King's belief in nonviolence was also an affirmation of the ultimate value of human life.

The Personal God of Love and Reason

According to personalism, reality can be understood best in terms of "personal" categories. Personalists had definite attributes in mind when they spoke of "personal" categories: spirit, mind, will, love, and reason. By using such categories, they intended to make it clear that personality cannot be defined correctly with the categories of space and time. Personality is not simply a "psycho-physical organism" (Brightman) and "personality and corporeality are incommensurable ideas" (Bowne). One cannot visibly see nor literally picture the essence of personality or self-hood — self-knowledge, self-control, and self-consciousness. One cannot likewise see ultimate reality, the Supreme Person. But the ground of all reality is "a supremely rational and supremely loving Person...God, the only Eternal Person."[30]

According to Brightman, " 'God is a spirit,' a being whose *esse* is to be conscious, to experience, to think, to will, to love, and to control the ongoing of the universe by rational purpose."[31] Further, Brightman contended that there is empirical evidence to support a belief in the existence of such a Being. First, the universe is characterized by order and purpose. Second, history points to the gradual realization of the ideals of cooperation and benevolence. Both of these facts are evidence of the work of a Supreme Mind whose purpose is the actualization of values. "Value," Brightman concluded, "is inherently a personal experience; and if the cosmic source of value is itself a value, it must be a person realizing ideals."[32]

When Brightman explained more fully the major attributes of a personal God, he argued that in the interpretation of God in the New Testament there are two traits that stand out above all others: reason (*logos*) and love (*agape*), or more accurately, "reasonable love." "There are," he explained, "at least two fundamentally unchangeable goals of all human action. They may be called intelligence and cooperation, or respect for truth and respect for personality, or reason and love...."[33] The universe is fundamentally rational and benevolent notwithstanding temporary aberrations and demonic impulses.

Reason and love, in Brightman's mind, are the "noblest powers" of the world of persons. The goal of life is the maximum development of those values, so that persons live together cooperatively and harmoniously. Even though human knowledge is often subject to error and is frequently incomplete, there is a distinction between the relatively less certain and the relatively more certain. Some human beliefs, when shown to be inadequate or subject to error, may not make an appreciable difference in one's understanding of human existence. However, some convictions are so fundamental and so crucial to understanding that, if they were proved false, no amount of readjustment would suffice to restore harmony and meaning to life. Reason and love are such convictions.

Reason and love are absolute norms and "fixed ends." If reason were not an absolute, science would be impossible; if love (i.e., respect for personality) were not an absolute, all value would be eliminated. If reason and love were universally sought as "fixed ends," they would produce unity and peace. Brightman suggested that the norms of reason and love have universal appeal to all races and creeds; they appear under different names in most philosophical systems and religious traditions. Although no one is completely reasonable and loving, reason and love point to the direction humanity must move if it is to avoid extinction. With this emphasis Brightman is representative of the best of liberal thought. His view of God is the basis of his optimistic assumptions shared by King. King's confidence in the success of nonviolence was predicated upon his conviction that a reasonable and loving God acts in history to assure justice and freedom.

Martin Luther King formulated his interpretation of God while writing his doctoral dissertation at Boston University. It was entitled "A Comparison of the Conceptions of God in the

Thinking of Paul Tillich and Henry Nelson Wieman." The study is an extensive exposition and comparison of the doctrines of God as held by Wieman and Tillich and a rigorous criticism of their views. His criticisms reflect the direct influence of the metaphysics of personalism, though he rejected Brightman's conception of a "finite" God. Brightman held that while God's goodness (love) is infinite, God's power is limited. Other personalists, like DeWolf, affirmed that both God's goodness and power are unlimited. King followed DeWolf in affirming both the omnipotence and the love of God.[34]

King disavowed Wieman's description of God as "integrating process" because a process is unconscious and impersonal. By way of contrast, two prerequisites of the personalist's God are consciousness and personality. King also rejected Tillich's conception of God as "Being-itself" because Tillich ascribed personality only to beings, not to Being (God). King was not impressed with Tillich's view of God as "supra-personal" or the Ground of the personal. King explained:

> Certainly it seems more empirical to ascribe personality to God than to ascribe "supra-personality" to him. In the world of experience the basic source of personality production and sustenance has been personality. Now when we are confronted with the fact of personality production and sustenance on a cosmic scale, why not ascribe the source to cosmic personality? It would be better by far to admit that there are difficulties with an idea we know — such as personality — than to employ a term which is practically unknown to us in our experience.[35]

King could not fathom why Wieman and Tillich insisted that to ascribe personality to God connotes a limitation and is thus an inappropriate symbol. He felt that their arguments were predicated upon an erroneous understanding of personality. He conceded "that human personality is limited, but personality as such involves no necessary limitation. It means simply self-consciousness and self-direction."[36] King supported his position by appealing to Borden Parker Bowne:

We must say with Bowne "that complete and perfect personality can be found only in the Infinite and Absolute Being, as only in him can we find complete and perfect selfhood and self-expression which is necessary to the fulness of personality." The conception of God as personal, therefore, does not imply limitation of any kind.[37]

In the effort to support further his belief in a personal God of love and reason, King contended that Christianity has always emphasized fellowship with God and trust in God's goodness. Both beliefs imply that God has a personal character. Fellowship can take place only between free and intelligent beings who know each other and have a mutual respect for each other. It is thus no surprise that he rejected Wieman's interpretation of God as "integrating process" and Tillich's as "Being-itself." Fellowship with an impersonal process and an abstract concept is impossible.

In like fashion King argued that only a personal God can be good and loving; impersonal goodness and love are inconceivable. Although Wieman and Tillich may speak of God's goodness and love, insofar as they deny the personality of God, their conceptions of goodness and love are abstract categories that do not allow fellowship with God. In counterdistinction to Wieman and Tillich, King conceived of God as a personal being of infinite love and limitless power and the creator and sustainer of value. "Christianity affirms that at the heart of reality is a Heart, a loving Father who works through history for the salvation of his children."[38]

A personal confession in *Strength to Love* is King's most persuasive statement of his belief in a personal God. The key passage is couched in deeply moving tones. He recalled that although he had accepted the concept of a personal God from an intellectual point of view for a long time, it was during the civil rights struggle — with the many harried days and nights, with the threats upon the life of himself and his family — that God became a living reality. He described his existential experience as follows:

I am convinced that the universe is under the control of a loving purpose, and that in the struggle for righteousness man has cosmic companionship. Behind the harsh appearances of the world there is a benign power. To say that this God is personal is not to make him a finite object beside other objects or attribute to him the limitations of human personality; it is to take what is finest and noblest in our consciousness and affirm its perfect existence in him.... So in the truest sense of the word, God is a living God. In him there is feeling and will, responsive to the deepest yearnings of the human heart: *this* God both evokes and answers prayer.[39]

The Moral Law

Another major theme of personalism that influenced King is the existence of an objective moral law in the universe which human beings should obey. That theme was described with clarity and precision by Brightman. He explained:

Idealists hold that moral experience points to an objective moral order in reality, as truly as sense experience points to an objective physical order, and most idealists believe that the objective existence of both orders can be understood rationally only if both are the activity or thought or experience of a supreme mind that generates the whole cosmic process and controls its ongoing.[40]

The moral law is a universal norm which human beings should use as the basis of decisions. By virtue of being a universal norm, it is a law; since it requires the will to choose, it is moral. The moral law is a manifestation of ultimate reality. It is not made by human beings; it is discovered by them.

In the thought of Brightman there is a direct relationship between God and the moral law of the universe. Without the existence of God, the moral order would collapse and ideals would be obliterated. The moral law is grounded in the nature of God. A god without moral concern might be all-powerful and all-knowing, but it could never be an object of religious faith. Religious faith is primarily concerned with the moral character of God. In short, the moral nature of the universe presupposes a moral author. According to Brightman:

> If religion be defined as co-operation between man and his God,
> expressed both in worship and in the conduct of life, then two
> important implications follow at once: First, that God is regarded
> as the embodiment of the moral ideal, and, secondly, that he
> is viewed as the very source or creator of a moral order in the
> universe.[41]

It is equally clear that for personalists there is a close relationship between metaphysics and ethics. Theistic metaphysics
provides a foundation for ethics, and ethics furnishes metaphysics
with practical content. Metaphysics deals with the divine nature;
ethics is concerned with the divine will. All of the personalists
who influenced King had a profound interest in ethics. This is
seen in the titles of some of their most important books: Borden
Parker Bowne, *The Principles of Ethics*; Edgar Sheffield Brightman,
Nature and Values and *Moral Laws*; Albert C. Knudson, *The Principles of Christian Ethics*; Peter Bertocci, *The Human Venture in
Sex, Love, and Marriage*; L. Harold DeWolf, *Responsible Freedom*.
These scholars, believing firmly in the moral law of the cosmos,
have attempted to grapple seriously with both the personal and
social significance of the moral life. Knudson concluded, for example, that given the three main arguments for the existence of
God — the ontological, teleological, and the moral — personalism opts for the moral because "all religion is based on faith in
the goodness of the world-ground."[42]

It is understandable, given King's debt to the prophetic model
of religion of Rauschenbusch, that personalism's emphasis upon
the existence of a moral law of the cosmos would appeal to King.
He insisted upon the moral foundation of reality. That belief is
perhaps more central and determinative for his thought than any
other. The interrelationship between the metaphysical and the
ethical is repeatedly manifested in King's thought in such key
phrases as "all reality hinges on moral foundations," "some creative force that works for universal wholeness," and "something
in history operating for good." Such phrases represent the combination of the metaphysics of personalism and the ethics of the
Hebrew prophets and Jesus. In spite of his recognition of the

forces of evil, King was able to press on because of his firm belief that good will ultimately triumph over evil, and love will eventually be victorious over injustice. "God," he affirmed, "is able to conquer the evils of history. . . . He has placed within the very structure of this universe certain absolute moral laws."[43] King saw evidence for this conviction in the fact that "when men and governments work devotedly for the good of others, they achieve their own enrichment in the process."[44]

King linked his belief in the moral law of the cosmos with the cross of Jesus Christ, the supreme manifestation of love. The cross is a "telescope" through which love is viewed. Love is the essence of the moral law, and thus the moral law supports the principle of the inherent value of human personality. For this reason, King insisted that civil rights is not a peripheral issue to be manipulated by self-seeking and unscrupulous politicians, but it is a theological and moral issue. Opposition to segregation and discrimination is not only demanded by the noble principles of democracy; it is also a response to the law of God. Black people should be given their freedom not because it is politically expedient but because the moral law of the cosmos demands it. God acts in history to assure the triumph of love and justice. "There is a creative power that works to pull down mountains of evil and level hilltops of injustice. God still works through history His wonders to perform."[45]

The Exodus event was appropriated by King as the model of the way God acts in history. Although evil may be recalcitrant and often appears to be the dominant force in human affairs, there is a "checkpoint in history." Such a checkpoint was demonstrated by the confrontation between Moses and Pharaoh and in the ensuing conflict between the Israelites and the Egyptians. The Red Sea destroyed Egyptian bondage, an evil that could not prevail against the will of God. King writes with confidence:

> A Red Sea passage in history ultimately brings the forces of goodness to victory, and the closing of the same waters marks the doom and destruction of the forces of evil. . . .

> All of this reminds us that evil carries the seed of its own destruction.... It [evil] can go a long way, but then it reaches its limit.[46]

King interpreted Napoleon's defeat at Waterloo in a similar way. Napoleon lost not because of superior military strength but because he acted contrary to the moral law of the cosmos. Waterloo is a symbol of the eternal truth "that in the long run of history might does not make right and the power of the sword cannot conquer the power of the spirit."[47]

The civil rights movement was seen by King as another illustration of the activity of God in history and the operation of the moral law. The movement was conceived as a manifestation of a transcendent and divine force. It made little difference to King how such a force is labeled. It may be called Whitehead's "principle of concretion," Wieman's "process of integration," Tillich's "Being-itself," or King's own conception of a personal God of love and reason. Regardless of the terminology, history testifies to the fact that "there is a creative force in this universe that works to bring the disconnected aspects of reality into a harmonious whole."[48] King saw the civil rights movement as God's answer to the injustices of segregation and discrimination. The belief in a personal God who holds the reins of history led many disadvantaged and disinherited people to adhere to nonviolence. It gave them an unshakable hope and a faith in the future. It was the reason they could accept suffering without retaliation. They were able to sing "We Shall Overcome" because they were convinced that although "the arc of the moral universe is long, it bends toward justice."[49]

The Social Nature of Human Existence and Community

In the thought of personalist philosophers there is an inseparable connection between the personal and social aspects of life. "Men," Knudson wrote, "are born to live together, and apart from this togetherness would not be truly human."[50] "The maxim 'Think for yourself,'" Brightman stated, "is basic; but the further maxim 'Think socially' must be added if philosophy is to do its whole duty."[51] The implication is that the nature of human beings is such that they need fellowship and thus they naturally seek community. Individuals are constantly interacting with each other in society, and such interaction affects their experience, consciousness, and history. An individual reaches the level of personhood only in social relations, a person develops and grows through social interaction with other persons. Hence, persons become mutually dependent — they need and rely upon each other. Knudson thought that this is the way life should be according to Christianity. "The real Christian world," he explained, "is a world of mutually dependent beings. It is a social world, a world of interacting moral beings; and in such a world love is necessarily the basic moral law."[52]

The social nature of human existence, according to personalism, is grounded in the nature of the Divine Personality. Although God does not need persons in order to exist, it is also true that God's "moral nature is love, and love needs comradeship. God . . . is not a solitary, self-enjoying mind. He is love; He is . . . the Great Companion."[53] The Christian community was the product of a human response to God's love. An inclusive human community should be the goal of social life. For this reason, social experiments which attempt to create inclusive human communities, such as democracy, should be viewed as attempts to live politically in tune with God's moral law.

Brightman saw the future as open to indeterminate possibilities because of his belief in "the inexhaustible perfectibility" of human nature. He was aware, given the reluctance of human beings to respond fully to reason and love, that the realization of an inclusive human community lies in the future. But his faith in human perfectibility gave him hope. Brightman's hope for the possibility of a universal human community was related to his belief in the inherent worth of personality. As long as there is respect for personality, there is hope for human unity — a unity that does not preclude or repress human differences of any kind. Although Brightman felt that the teachings of Jesus were gradually being manifested in democracy, he hastened to add that humankind still has a great deal to learn about love and justice.

The method Brightman advocated to achieve an inclusive human community was cooperation. In his mind, cooperation is the essence of both religion and ethics. In the first place, religion is cooperation with God; unless there is a human response to God, there is no such thing as religion. A response to God involves cooperation with God's purposes for human life, including respect for personality. Thus, in the second place, religion involves cooperation between human beings to foster and to conserve personal values. When human beings refuse to cooperate for the realization of personal values, they are refusing to cooperate with God's will. As a result of cooperation, human beings are liberated from selfishness, and they are able to open themselves to the needs of their neighbors. In other words, Brightman suggested that the success of his method will depend upon an appeal to the best in human beings — their sense of fairness, rationality, and spiritual sensitivity. Plato called this method "persuasion" and Christianity called it "conversion." Brightman prefers to use the term "rational love in education." The concepts Brightman employed to describe the ideal human community, such as inclusiveness, cooperation, and unity, are very prominent in King's vision of the Beloved Community — the subject of the next chapter.

THE INFLUENCE OF HEGEL

The philosophy of Georg Friedrich Hegel (1770–1831) was another subject that King studied at Boston University that was very important in his intellectual pilgrimage. King had been introduced to Hegel in survey courses in philosophy in undergraduate (Morehouse) and graduate (University of Pennsylvania) schools. However, his first intensive study of Hegel occurred in a seminar at Boston University that extended over an entire year. Brightman regularly taught the seminar on Hegel, and King was enrolled in it during the academic year of 1952–1953. When Brightman became ill the first semester and did not return to teach, Peter Bertocci finished the seminar in Brightman's absence.

The major text in the course was Hegel's *Phenomenology of Mind*, and King recalled that he also read Hegel's *Philosophy of History* and *Philosophy of Right*.[54] Peter Bertocci recalls that King, usually quiet in class, became quite interested when his fellow students began to discuss Hegel's interpretation of the relationship between master and slave. He was fascinated by Hegel's argument that a master could become so dependent upon a slave that a slave could assume the dominant role in the relationship.[55] This was apparently the incident that ignited King's interest in Hegel's dialectical method of thinking. According to Hegel, the self ascertains truth through the introduction of opposites (i.e., a thesis and an antithesis) and the combination of them into a synthesis. Every truth is the synthesis of two seemingly contradictory elements. Every affirmation implies a negation; every "yes" implies a "no." Truth is the product of a synthesis of an affirmation and the negation. The historical process is also characterized by the constant emergence of theses, antitheses, and syntheses.

It is important to point out that it was primarily Hegel's dialectical method, not Hegel's metaphysics (i.e., absolute idealism), that influenced King. King flatly rejected Hegel's metaphysics on the grounds that it "was rationally unsound ... because it tended to swallow up the many in the one."[56] At every point where there was an essential difference between Hegel's absolute idealism and personalism, King came down on the side of personalism. At the same time, the Hegelian methodology pervaded King's thinking and writing. At the outset of *Strength to Love* he said: " ... life at its best is a creative synthesis of opposites in fruitful harmony. The philosopher Hegel said that truth is found neither in the thesis nor the antithesis, but in an emergent synthesis which reconciles the two."[57]

The following quotations are examples of how King used the dialectical method as he grappled with certain knotty subjects:

> The Kingdom of God is neither the thesis of individual enterprise nor the antithesis of collective enterprise, but a synthesis which reconciles the truth of both.[58]

> An adequate understanding of man is found neither in the thesis of liberalism nor in the antithesis of neoorthodoxy, but in a synthesis which reconciles the truths of both.[59]

> The third way open to oppressed people in their quest for freedom is the way of nonviolent resistance. Like the synthesis in Hegelian philosophy, the principle of nonviolent resistance seeks to reconcile the truths of two opposites — acquiescence and violence — while avoiding the extremes and immoralities of both.[60]

> …the truth about man is found neither in the thesis of pessimistic materialism nor the antithesis of optimistic humanism, but in a higher synthesis. Man is neither villain nor hero; he is rather both villain and hero.[61]

Unfortunately, King did not always spell out clearly what he meant by the synthesis, in spite of the fact that it was obviously his position.

In addition to Hegel's methodology, King was also impressed with the teleological character of Hegel's thought and his emphasis that "growth comes through struggle."[62] These aspects of Hegel's thought are reflected in the fact that King set the Montgomery bus boycott and the civil rights movement within the framework of God's activity to effect social change within history. In an address at the First Annual Institute on Nonviolence and Social Change in Montgomery, Alabama, in December 1965, he said: "We stand today between two worlds — the dying old and the emerging new." When he explained, he drew upon his philosophical training:

> Long ago the Greek philosopher Heraclitus argued that justice emerges from the strife of opposites, and Hegel, in modern philosophy, preached a doctrine of growth through struggle. It is both historically and biologically true that there can be no birth and growth without birth and growing pains.[63]

King refused to accept the Montgomery boycott and the subsequent civil rights movement as isolated events. That is, he
viewed them as integral parts of an evolving historical process
whose ultimate goals are freedom and justice. Thus, when he
spoke at the fourth anniversary of the Montgomery Improvement
Association on December 3, 1959, he remarked that he did not
have to create unity because the organization had been created
by the processes of history.

The arrest of Rosa Parks, the event that precipitated the
Montgomery bus boycott, was also viewed by King as a manifestation of a moral process gradually unfolding within history. In
his words:

> She was anchored to that seat by the accumulated indignities of
> days gone by and the boundless aspirations of generations yet un-
> born. She was a victim of both the forces of history and the forces
> of destiny. She had been tracked down by the *Zeitgeist* — the spirit
> of the time.[64]

As a result of the moral order of the universe, the yearning for
freedom and justice by an oppressed people eventually comes to
the surface and cannot be ignored. Black people in the United
States have been caught up in the *Zeitgeist* that is prompting all
oppressed people to struggle for liberation and justice. The *Zeitgeist* has forced upon this generation "an indescribably important
destiny — to complete a process of democratization which our
nation has too long developed too slowly...."[65]

It is clear that King saw polarities in every situation, but he
hoped they would be brought together in a synthesis. Theologi-
cally speaking, his goal was reconciliation. This is evident in the
way he interpreted the progress of race relations in the United
States. He disagreed with the optimists who felt that the race
problem would be solved soon because great progress has been
made; he disagreed with the pessimists who claimed that virtually
nothing had been accomplished and that integration would be
impossible. King advocated a third position, which he called "the
realistic attitude." "Like the synthesis of Hegelian philosophy," he

explained, "the realistic attitude seeks to reconcile the truths of two opposites and avoid the extremes of both."[66] According to realism, some progress has been made, but there is still a long way to go. In other words, he saw the history of race relations in the United States from an evolutionary perspective — a gradual development from slavery to segregation, from segregation to desegregation, from desegregation to integration. Such a development shows that the process of history continues to unfold; it is moving toward an inclusive human community which will be characterized by love, peace, justice, freedom, and equality.

However, King did not believe that social conditions would be improved automatically. Time, in fact, might be the ally of the status quo. King argued instead that social change would be the result of human responsiveness to the *Zeitgeist*. Moreover, he was aware that such a response often produces tension and conflict. For example, progress was achieved in many Southern communities only after the powerful social, political, and economic structures (i.e., a thesis) were confronted by a united, committed, oppressed people (i.e., an antithesis). As a result of tension and conflict, a synthesis emerged — a new reality that combined the best in each position. A qualitative leap forward in history is usually accompanied by conflict and suffering.

The influence of the Hegelian methodology is manifested in King's attempt to avoid extreme positions. He was inclined toward mediation and conciliation. For instance, he wished to avoid the position of both the revolutionary and the moderate, the sources of gradualism and directionless spontaneity, and the defeatism of both acquiescence ("Uncle Tomism") and violence ("hotheadedness"). Further, he endorsed education and legislation, on the one hand, and nonviolent direct action, on the other hand, as viable means of social change. It is understandable then that King was uncomfortable with the Black Power movement as exemplified by Stokely Carmichael. He saw both black power and white supremacy as extreme points of view. A creative synthesis, in his mind, had to emerge from the thesis of one view and the antithesis of the other.

Although Martin Luther King was influenced significantly by Hegel's dialectical method of thinking and his teleological interpretation of history, he did not accept Hegel's world view. Hegel's Absolute Idea was far removed from King's conception of the biblical God of the Exodus and the cross who is active in history to deliver God's people from bondage to freedom.

CHAPTER SIX

The Vision of
the Beloved Community

I N THE FOREGOING PAGES the concept of the Beloved Community has been alluded to again and again. We are now in a position to examine that concept as the capstone of King's thought. The vision of the Beloved Community was the organizing principle of all of King's thought and activity. His writings and his involvement in the civil rights movement were illustrations of and footnotes to his fundamental preoccupation with the actualization of an inclusive human community. According to King, the "most creative turn of events" in humanity's long history occurred when humans gave up their stone axes and began to cooperate with their neighbors. King explained:

That seemingly elementary decision set in motion what we know now as civilization. At the heart of all that civilization has meant and developed is "community" — the mutually cooperative and voluntary venture of man to assume a semblance of responsibility for his brother.[1]

All of King's elementary concerns were directly related to the priority he assigned to the Beloved Community. Liberalism and personalism provided the theological and philosophical foundations of the concept; nonviolence provided the means to attain it; the Christian realism of Reinhold Niebuhr qualified King's initial optimism about the possibility of actualizing it within history and changed King's attitude about the kinds of tactics necessary to move toward it. The centrality of the Beloved Community in King's intellectual concerns is demonstrated by the fact that it can be traced from his earliest addresses and articles to his latest writings and public speeches. In one of his first articles he stated that the purpose of the Montgomery bus boycott "is reconciliation; the end is redemption; the end is the creation of the beloved community."[2] In his last book he wrote, "Our loyalties must transcend our race, our tribe, our class, and our nation...."[3] This was King's way of stating that the crux of his faith was a vision of a completely integrated society, a community of love and justice. In his mind, such a community would be the ideal corporate expression of the Christian faith.

THE MEANING OF
THE BELOVED COMMUNITY

King's conception of the Beloved Community is best described as a transformed and regenerated human society. In the newsletter of the Southern Christian Leadership Conference in 1957, shortly after the new civil rights organization had been formed, King described its purpose and goal as follows: "The ultimate aim of SCLC is to foster and create the 'beloved community' in America where brotherhood is a reality....SCLC works for integration. Our ultimate goal is genuine intergroup and interpersonal living — *integration*."[4] As this description indicates, King conceived the Beloved Community in terms of an integrated society wherein unity would be an actuality in every aspect of social life.

Integration, according to King, was a much more inclusive and positive concept than desegregation. Desegregation is essentially negative in the sense that it eliminates discrimination against blacks in public accommodations, education, housing, and employment — those aspects of social life that can be corrected by laws. By way of contrast, integration means "the positive acceptance of desegregation and the welcomed participation of Negroes into the total range of human activities...."[5] But King did not believe that the transition from desegregation to integration would be inevitable or automatic. Whereas desegregation can be accomplished by laws, integration will require a change in attitudes, the loving acceptance of individuals and groups.

Integration, as King understood it, involves personal and social relationships that are created by love. Therefore, an integrated society cannot be legislated. When segregation has been abolished and desegregation has been accomplished, blacks and whites will then have to learn to relate to each other across those nonrational, psychological barriers which have traditionally separated them in our society. Everyone will have to become color-blind. Desegregation, King explained, will only create "a society where men are physically desegregated and spiritually segregated, where elbows are together and hearts apart. It gives us social togetherness and spiritual apartness. It leaves us with a stagnant equality of sameness rather than a constructive equality of oneness."[6] Integration will produce an entirely different kind of society whose character is best expressed in the theme "Black and White Together," the title of one of the chapters of *Why We Can't Wait* and one of the verses of the hymn of the civil rights movement, "We Shall Overcome." Integration will enlarge "the concept of brotherhood to a vision of total interrelatedness."[7]

As the emphasis upon interrelatedness suggests, King's conception of the Beloved Community assumed a theme mentioned throughout these pages, the social nature of human existence. The phrase King used to express this theme was "the solidarity of the human family." Everyone who is even slightly acquainted with King's writings and speeches is familiar with the words, "We are tied together in the single garment of destiny, caught in an inescapable network of mutuality."[8] This was King's homiletical way of affirming that reality is composed of structures that form an interrelated whole. That is to say, people are dependent upon each other. Whatever one is or possesses, one owes to many others who have preceded him. "Whether we realize it or not," King wrote, "each of us lives eternally 'in the red.' "[9] The recognition of one's indebtedness to others should destroy the attitude of self-sufficiency so often characteristic of human nature and should lead to an awareness that individuals need each other for human fulfillment. Individual maturity and personal growth cannot take place apart from meaningful relationships with other persons. The interrelated and interdependent character of life means that the "I" cannot attain fulfillment without the "Thou." Selves who recognize their interdependency must be nurtured in order for the Beloved Community to emerge.

Significant insights can be gained into King's interpretation of the Beloved Community when it is realized that he viewed the composition of the civil rights movement as a microcosm of the Beloved Community. The people who attended the mass meetings and rallies, who participated in the demonstrations, and who worked in other innumerable ways were from every segment of American society. Professional leaders (teachers, lawyers, doctors, clergy, etc.) willingly walked and worked with domestics and day laborers. Every social class and every age group was represented. The educated and the illiterate, the affluent and the welfare recipient, white and black — people who had heretofore been separated by rigid social mores and laws — were brought together in a common cause.

After the March to Montgomery in the spring of 1966, several thousand people were delayed at the airport because their planes were late. King was so impressed by the heterogeneity yet the obvious unity of the crowd that he remarked:

> As I stood with them and saw white and Negro, nuns and priests, ministers and rabbis, labor organizers, lawyers, doctors, housemaids and shopworkers brimming with vitality and enjoying a rare comradeship, I knew I was seeing a microcosm of the mankind of the future in this moment of luminous and genuine brotherhood.[10]

King frequently called upon whites to help in his various campaigns. He attempted to make the base of the movement as broad and as universal as possible. He saw the movement as a preview of the interrelatedness of human existence that would characterize the Beloved Community.

King interpreted the interrelatedness of human existence to mean that "injustice anywhere is a threat to justice everywhere" because injustice has a corporate effect. He believed that the denial of constitutional rights to anyone potentially violated the rights of all citizens. The victim of electric cattle prods and biting police dogs was the entire national community. Discrimination against 10 percent of the population of the United States weakens the whole social fabric. The issues of race and poverty are not merely sectional problems; they are American problems. Thus it follows, according to King, that the liberation of black people will also lead to the emancipation of white people. He took seriously the indivisibility of human existence. He concluded:

> In a real sense all life is interrelated. The agony of the poor impoverishes the rich; the betterment of the poor enriches the rich. We are inevitably our brother's keeper because we are our brother's brother. Whatever affects one directly affects all indirectly.[11]

As a result of his solidaristic approach to human existence, King believed that the civil rights movement was contributing more to the national life than simply the elimination of racial injustice. Although integration is usually associated solely with the struggle for racial equality, King conceived integration in a much broader way. King's vision of the future included a society which would be free not only from the malformation of persons resulting from racial hatred but also free from the abnormality of persons resulting from economic injustice and exploitation. That is, King was not interested in justice for blacks in opposition to justice for whites; he was concerned about justice for everyone.

What King had in mind when he spoke about justice for everyone is perfectly clear. He wrote:

> Let us be dissatisfied until rat-infested, vermin-filled slums will be a thing of a dark past and every family will have a decent sanitary house in which to live. Let us be dissatisfied until the empty stomachs of Mississippi are filled and the idle industries of Appalachia are revitalized.... Let us be dissatisfied until our brothers of the Third World — Asia, Africa and Latin America — will no longer be the victim of imperialist exploitation, but will be lifted from the long night of poverty, illiteracy and disease.[12]

It is equally clear that when King spoke about justice he included all the poor — blacks; whites; Hispanic, Asian, and native
Americans. The vision of economic justice is a possession and a
right of the whole human race. Furthermore, King was aware that
in order to actualize that vision, the structures of economic injustice so characteristic of capitalism had to be eliminated and
supplanted by those that would produce economic justice.

King's views on economic justice and its importance for an
inclusive human community reflect an early and consistent concern of King for an egalitarian, socialistic approach to wealth and
property. "A life," he wrote, "is sacred. Property is intended to
serve life, and no matter how much we surround it with rights
and respect, it has no personal being. It is part of the earth man
walks on; it is not man."[13] King frequently chastised the United
States for its economic system which withheld the necessities of
life from the masses while allowing luxuries to be monopolized
by the few. He believed fervently that one of the major goals
of the United States should be to bridge the gap between ab-
ject poverty and inordinate wealth. The Beloved Community, in
King's mind, would be a manifestation of God's intention that
everyone should have the physical and spiritual necessities of
life. To this end, during the latter part of his life, he began
to advocate a variety of economic programs, including the creation of jobs by government and the institution of a guaranteed
annual minimal income. The noble thoughts expressed in the
famous "Dream Speech" during the March on Washington in
August 1963 were more than rhetoric for King. He was impatient with such phrases as "human dignity" and "brotherhood of
man" if they did not find concrete expression in the structures
of society.

King arrived at his egalitarian position on wealth very early
in life, and it was directly related to his strong feelings about
racial discrimination. Although his economic views were later
influenced by the thought of Karl Marx, King was not a Marxist. He studied Marx and other critics of capitalism in one of
his courses on Christian ethics with one of the authors. In the

course called "Christian Social Philosophy II," described earlier, King gave an oral report in class on Max Weber's *The Protestant Ethic and the Spirit of Capitalism* and Richard Tawney's *Religion and the Rise of Capitalism*. King later told one of the authors that he had chosen those books from the reading list provided because he had been concerned from an early age about economic injustice and critical of laissez-faire capitalism, and he wished to find out what Protestantism had contributed to the rise of a system that had kept the poor, especially blacks, in bondage to the ideology of Adam Smith. He elaborated upon this theme in *Strength to Love:*

> During my early teens I was deeply concerned by the problem of racial justice.... The first time that I was seated behind a curtain in a dining car I felt as though the curtain had been dropped on my selfhood. I also learned that the inseparable twin of racial injustice is economic injustice. I saw how the systems of segregation exploited both the Negro and the poor whites. These early experiences made me deeply conscious of the varieties of injustice in our society.[14]

King had studied Karl Marx before enrolling in "Christian Social Philosophy II." He recalled:

> During the Christmas holidays of 1949 I decided to spend my spare time reading Karl Marx to try to understand the appeal of communism for many people. For the first time I carefully scrutinized *Das Kapital* and *The Communist Manifesto.* I also read some interpretive works on the thinking of Marx and Lenin.[15]

King read Marx at that particular time because he was enrolled in a course on "Philosophy of History" at the University of Pennsylvania, and Marx was one of the major figures studied.

A major section of "Christian Social Philosophy II" was devoted to the neo-Protestant critique of Western culture as stated primarily by Paul Tillich in *The Religious Situation* and *The Protestant Era* and by Reinhold Niebuhr in *Moral Man and Immoral Society* and *Reflections on the End of an Era.* The early works of Tillich and Niebuhr had been strongly influenced by Marx;

therefore, the students were also encouraged to read some of the works of Marx in order to comprehend Tillich and Niebuhr. Marxist themes, such as the critique of bourgeois culture and laissez-faire capitalism, are found in almost everyone who takes Niebuhr and Tillich seriously. King was no exception though he did not accept Marx's world view. After pointing out how his thinking had been stimulated by Marx, King observed:

> In so far as Marx posited a metaphysical materialism, an ethical relativism, and a strangulating totalitarianism, I responded with an unambiguous "no"; but in so far as he pointed to weaknesses of traditional capitalism, contributed to the growth of a definite self-consciousness in the masses, and challenged the social conscience of the Christian churches, I responded with a definite "yes."[16]

That King was influenced by Karl Marx is beyond doubt, but the extent of Marx's influence has been overestimated both by his critics who would like to pin the Communist label on him and by some of his supporters who would like to claim him for the "New Left." Both of these groups have missed the point because there are bases in Christian theology and ethics to support the position King adopted regarding Marxism. He wrote:

> We must ... recognize that truth is not to be found either in traditional capitalism or in Marxism. Each represents a partial truth. Historically, capitalism failed to discern the truth in collective enterprise and Marxism failed to see the truth in individual enterprise. Nineteenth-century capitalism failed to appreciate that life is social, and Marxism failed ... to see that life is individual and social. The Kingdom of God is neither the thesis of individual enterprise nor the antithesis of collective enterprise, but a synthesis which reconciles the truth of both.[17]

It seems that King's synthesis was evolutionary or democratic socialism, though he never used those terms — he evidently felt that was one epithet he could forego. At any rate, King did not have to be a Marxist to advocate "radical" and "revolutionary" views on economic justice. Many of Reinhold Niebuhr's works, such as *The Nature and Destiny of Man, Faith and History, The Children of Light and the Children of Darkness,* contain a thoroughgoing critique of Marxism while supporting an egalitarian approach to wealth and property on the basis of a distinctly Christian interpretation of humanity and history. King also believed that Christianity, properly conceived, is a radical and revolutionary faith.

The point is that King could not envision the Beloved Community apart from the alleviation of economic inequity and the achievement of economic justice. Harvey Cox has aptly pointed out that with this emphasis King combined two traditional biblical themes, the "holiness of the poor" and the "blessed community." In the movement which King led, blacks became the embodiment of "the poor" and integration represented the vision of "the holy community." Cox explains:

> It is...essential to notice that the two elements, the holy outcast *and* the blessed community, must go together. Without the vision of restored community, the holiness ascribed to the poor would fall far short of politics and result in a mere perpetuation of charity and service activities.[18]

King's vision of the Beloved Community included all races, all classes, all ethnic groups, all nations, and all religions.

THE BELOVED COMMUNITY AND THE AMERICAN DREAM

The event in the life of Martin Luther King which is probably remembered by more people than any other is his "I Have a Dream" speech, delivered during the March on Washington on August 28, 1963. However, the major motifs of that speech, as was the case for many of King's other well-known themes, were first formulated while he was pastor of the Dexter Avenue Baptist Church in Montgomery, Alabama, and during the Montgomery bus boycott (1955–1957). Be that as it may, the figure of the Dream was used by King to portray in a dramatic way his vision of the Beloved Community. The best succinct statement of King's conception of the Dream in concrete terms is contained in the following passage:

> The dream is one of equality of opportunity, of privilege and property widely distributed; a dream of a land where men will not take necessities from the many to give luxuries to the few; a dream of a land where men do not argue that the color of a man's skin determines the content of his character; a dream of a place where all our gifts and resources are held not for ourselves alone but as instruments of service for the rest of humanity; the dream of a country where every man will respect the dignity and worth of all human personality, and men will dare to live together as brothers.... Whenever it is fulfilled, we will emerge from the bleak and desolate midnight of man's inhumanity to man into the bright and glowing daybreak of freedom and justice for all of God's children.[19]

As this statement indicates, King envisaged a new social order wherein all kinds of people and groups would live together as brothers and share equally the abundance of God's creation. Dr. L. Harold DeWolf explained to one of the authors that King believed that the Dream existed originally in the mind of God and that King saw himself as a medium for the communication of God's dream to God's people.[20] This belief, of course, was consistent with King's conception of the biblical God who had inspired the prophetic teachings of Amos, Micah, and Isaiah about justice, mercy, and peace.

King's vision of the Beloved Community, expressed in his Dream, was closely related to the perennial dream of American democracy. In the United States there has always been the dream of a future utopia or Holy Commonwealth, a dream of "a land of the free and the home of the brave" and "a land flowing with milk and honey." Such a dream has occupied a prominent place in both the political rhetoric and the religious symbolism of the United States. In other words, the American Dream has been derived from a combination of the religious hope for the kingdom of God of the Puritans and the secular dream of democracy rooted in the Enlightenment of the eighteenth century. The goal of both traditions has been a perfected society in which there would be opportunity and equality for all. The United States has been conceived of as a place where people of all backgrounds, creeds, and races would live harmoniously together — a micro-cosm of what humankind could be. It has not been uncommon throughout the history of the United States for Christianity to be identified with the ideals of democracy, and for democracy to be viewed as the social expression of Christianity.

It is clear that King shared the American Dream and that he associated the secular elements of the dream drawn from demo-cratic political theory and the religious elements derived from the Judeo-Christian faith. King readily confessed that his vision of the Beloved Community was "deeply rooted in the American dream."[21] His conception of these roots was expressed at Lincoln University in a commencement address in which he contended that "America is essentially a dream."

> It is a dream of a land where men of all races, of all nationalities, and of all creeds can live together as brothers. The substance of the dream is expressed in these sublime words, words lifted to cosmic proportions: "We hold these truths to be self-evident — that all men are created equal; that they are endowed by their Creator with certain inalienable rights; that among these are life, liberty, and the pursuit of happiness." This is the dream.[22]

Further, King highlighted two elements of the American Dream that seemed to him to be especially crucial. One of the elements is the universalism of the Dream. It includes all classes, races, and religions — rich and poor, black and white, Protes-tants, Catholics, and Jews. Another element of the Dream is that each person, by virtue of being a human being and a child of God, possesses certain inherent rights that are God-given and not simply privileges extended by the state. The rights of life, liberty, and the pursuit of happiness mean that all individuals everywhere should have "three meals a day for their bodies, ed-ucation and culture for their minds, and dignity, equality and freedom for their spirits."[23]

King saw the civil rights movement as an effort to recall the United States to its original dream and thereby to resolve what Gunnar Myrdal had called "the American Dilemma," the gap between America's professed ideals and actual practices. He believed that black people had a peculiar contribution to make to the revival of the American Dream. The black population of the United States will provide "a new expression of the American dream that need not be realized at the expense of other men around the world, but a dream of opportunity and life that can be shared with the rest of the world."[24] King stands in that long line of American prophets in whose minds the American Dream and the "Holy Commonwealth" have been virtually indistinguishable. "The Dream Speech" combines ideals from both secular democratic philosophy (i.e., freedom and equality for all) and the prophetic tradition of the Bible (i.e., the dignity of persons and justice equally distributed).

As a result of the centrality given to the American Dream and the dimensions he added to it, King not only challenged the United States to a renewed commitment to the ideals that had been professed by American democracy, he also transformed what has been called "the civil religion of America." John Dixon Elder explains:

> In a remarkable way, Martin Luther King served both as preacher to the people of his own Baptist tradition and as spokesman for an enlarged American civil religion. His sermons are filled with the biblical terminology that from the beginning was applied to the American national experience — the exodus, the wilderness, and the promised land. But King revived this terminology, making a fresh and profoundly meaningful application to our present national situation. Though he was speaking to black Americans of "going up on the mountain" and "looking over Jordan," his words rescued an inheritance of religious terminology for white Americans as well. In a day when the usefulness of "God talk" is widely questioned, King used the biblical symbols that are at the heart of American civil religion and gave them fresh meaning.[25]

Since King included blacks and other disinherited groups in his dream, he not only revived the American Dream, he also broadened it. It strikes Elder as ironic that King had to give his life in the attempt to achieve for black people those human rights already guaranteed in the Constitution and the Declaration of Independence. Nevertheless, the inclusion of blacks in the dream "enabled black Americans to shape the substance of a civil religion from which, ironically, they have been heretofore excluded."[26] By broadening the perimeters of American civil religion, King brought that religion closer to the Christian norm of community.[27] He had his moments of despair and doubt like all mortals, but he never lost hope that "there will be a great camp meeting in the promised land." The explanation for this fact is that King's vision of the Beloved Community was rooted not only in the American Dream, but, more importantly, it was rooted in his religious faith. James Cone is correct when he claims that King's dream was "grounded not in the hopes of white America but in God."[28] King's conception of the Beloved Community was grounded, in the final analysis, not in the tradition of the Enlightenment or secular democratic political theory but in the millennial hope of Judeo-Christian religion.

THE BELOVED COMMUNITY, THE KINGDOM OF GOD, AND THE MILLENNIAL HOPE

King's conception of the Beloved Community was fundamentally indebted to the scriptural view of the millennial hope. The belief in a millennial hope has been an integral part of the Jewish conception of the Messianic Era and the Christian doctrine of the kingdom of God. Although the doctrine of the kingdom of God did not occupy an explicit place in King's writings, it was obviously implicit in everything he said and did. The explanation for the lack of prominence of this doctrine undoubtedly lies in the fact that the kingdom of God and the Beloved Community were synonymous in King's thought. That this is the case is clearly demonstrated in the following passage, one of the few attempts he made to define what he meant by the kingdom of God.

> Jesus took over the phrase "the Kingdom of God," but he changed its meaning. He refused entirely to be the kind of a Messiah that

his contemporaries expected. Jesus made love the mark of sovereignty. Here we are left with no doubt as to Jesus' meaning. The Kingdom of God will be a society in which men and women live as children of God should live. It will be a kingdom controlled by the law of love.... Many have attempted to say that the ideal of a better world will be worked out in the next world. But Jesus taught men to say, "Thy will be done in earth, as it is in heaven." Although the world seems to be in a bad shape today, we must never lose faith in the power of God to achieve his purpose.[29]

This quotation indicates that there was a close relationship between King's conception of the kingdom of God and the Beloved Community as described earlier, just as he often associated his dream with the American Dream. Both the conception of the kingdom of God and the Beloved Community expressed, according to King, an optimism about the future of society and historical progress. Further, the phraseology that he used to explicate those concepts reflects his debt to the liberal interpretation of the millennial hope as found in the Hebrew prophets and Jesus.

Reinhold Niebuhr observed in one of King's favorite books, *Moral Man and Immoral Society*, that every religion which has been concerned to ameliorate the problems of society has also included a millennial hope — a vision of a "golden age" in the future wherein there would be great happiness, peace, justice, and prosperity. "The religious imagination," Niebuhr explained, "is as impatient with the compromises, relativities and imperfections of historic society as with the imperfections of individual life."[30] Hence, Israel's prophets looked toward the arrival of the Messianic Era, and Jesus proclaimed the advent of the kingdom of God. In the Judeo-Christian tradition the Messianic Era and the kingdom of God have included a concern for communal life, corporate faith, social justice, and a hope for a transformed society. King drew upon all of these themes in his description of the Beloved Community. When these themes are combined, they can be expressed succinctly in the familiar phrase "the fatherhood of God and the brotherhood of man," a phrase which represents the distillation of many of the theological presuppositions of liberalism, the social gospel, and personalism. For King, the most important theological presuppositions were the liberal version of the doctrine of creation, the prophetic appeal for social justice, and the New Testament concept of *agape*.

One of King's major theological presuppositions of the Beloved Community was the liberal version of the doctrine of creation. This doctrine meant, in King's thought, that all persons are created in the image of God and are therefore inseparably bound together. As he stated it: all persons are "made from the same basic stuff... molded in the same divine image."[31] The divine image in persons is the source of "humanness" or human identity — an identity that transcends distinctions between Jew and Gentile, black and white, Russian and American. "There is neither Jew nor Greek, there is neither bond nor free, there is neither male nor female: for ye are all one in Christ Jesus" (Galatians 3:28, KJV). King considered the universalism of this passage to be the heart of the Christian gospel. This universalism was his basis for contending that segregation is morally indefensible and integration is ethically unavoidable. Since all persons have one Creator, all human beings are brothers and sisters. The dignity and worth of every person are rooted in one's relationship as offspring of God. This relationship, held in common by all, is the source of unity and community.

Another theological presupposition of King's conception of the Beloved Community was the prophetic vision of justice, peace, freedom, equality, and harmony associated with the Messianic Era. King repeatedly drew upon the words of the Hebrew prophets in his appeal for social justice, and he understood religion in terms of the prophetic model as it had been stated by Walter Rauschenbusch.[32] King grasped the significance of history and ethics for the prophets' interpretation of religion, and their emphases were integral to his vision of the Beloved Community. In his view, Yahweh is a just and righteous God who requires justice and righteousness from his children. King did not spiritualize the demand of the prophets for justice by projecting it into the world-to-come. To the contrary, he spelled it out in terms of equality in voting, public accommodations, education, jobs, housing, and related concerns. In short, King conceived justice and righteousness in this-worldly terms, and he expected them to be achieved within history.

The third major theological source of King's conception of the Beloved Community was Christian love (*agape*). King defined *agape* as "redeeming good will for all men.... It is the love of God operating in the human heart."[33] *Agape* creates genuine personal relations between people, making them neighbors and friends. In other words, as King interpreted *agape*, it is linked with his conception of community. Love is a community-creating force; it is the only force that can bring community into existence because its inherent unselfishness leads to cooperation instead of competition and conflict. *Agape* will do whatever is necessary to originate and to perpetuate community. All human efforts to establish community are supported by the laws of the universe because God created the universe that way. By way of contrast, hate always destroys community because it depersonalizes people and thus makes genuine personal relations impossible. When human beings pervert or destroy community, they resist the laws of God's created order. The crucifixion-resurrection-Pentecost symbols of Christianity, according to King, point to the advent of the Beloved Community. He wrote:

> The cross is the eternal expression of the length to which God will go in order to restore broken community. The resurrection is a symbol of God's triumph over all the forces that seek to block community. The Holy Spirit is the continuing community creating reality that moves through history.[34]

Christian love can produce integration, not simply desegregation.

The foregoing analysis of King's conception of the Beloved Community indicates that Harvey Cox is on target when he contends that the Hebrew term *shalom* expresses what King had in mind. Cox reminds us that though *shalom* is usually translated "peace," it had a much broader connotation. He contends that *shalom* has three components, all of which were essential for

King's conception of the Beloved Community. The first component is reconciliation — an era in which all religious, racial, cultural, and political barriers will be broken down. The second component is freedom — an era wherein everyone will be liberated *from* bondage and be free *for* service and responsibility. The third component is hope — the expectation that God's world will be renewed.[35] By connecting *shalom* and Beloved Community, Cox has rightly understood that King was indebted primarily to biblical categories and not those of social and political philosophy. According to the biblical categories King utilized, religion and social issues are inextricably bound together.

MEANS TO ACHIEVE
THE BELOVED COMMUNITY

Chapter 3 has already presented what King meant by nonviolence; how nonviolence is related to Christian love; and that he viewed nonviolence as the means to achieve the Beloved Community. But there are ramifications of these elements of King's thought that need to be explicated further. Nonviolence, according to King, had a dual meaning: (1) It was "a way of life" (i.e., a religious and moral norm derived from *agape*). (2) It was "a method of action" (i.e., a strategy of social change).[36] The two elements of nonviolence were inseparable in King's thought and action. Although he was aware that many people associated with the civil rights movement accepted nonviolence only as "a method of action," King insisted that for him it was also "a way of life," and his actions unequivocally testified to that fact.

King conceived nonviolence as the only moral means to achieve the Beloved Community. Conversely, he considered violence to be both immoral and impractical. Violence is immoral because it is based upon hate instead of love; violence is impractical because it is counterproductive. King contended that the record of history showed that violence had usually been self-defeating. He admitted that some political change had been achieved by violence (e.g., the American Revolution), but he hastened to point out that the goal of the black revolution was integration, not independence. Whereas the goal of independence is usually the annihilation of the oppressor, the goal of integration is reconciliation. Such a goal can be achieved only through nonviolence. Love is the only force that can raise human relationships to the level of trust and understanding necessary to unite a fragmented society and to bring about the Beloved Community.

Further light may be shed upon King's insistence upon the inseparability of nonviolence as a norm and a strategy, if we consider how he conceived the perennial issue of the relationship between means and ends. King did not ask whether the end justifies the means, the classical way of stating the question. He argued that the goal determines the method. It was inconceivable to King that moral ends could be achieved by immoral means. Thus, it was only logical for him to conclude that it would be inconsistent to attempt to actualize the Beloved Community by any means except nonviolence. He apparently was cognizant of the fact that change agents are usually criticized more for their behavior (means) than for their goals. Most people feel that the behavior of people involved in a social movement should reflect the goals they are seeking to universalize. There was a consistency between King's personal lifestyle and strategy and his ultimate goal, the Beloved Community.

Although King made his personal position on the relationship between nonviolence as "a way of life" and "a method of action" perfectly clear, he did not expect or insist that everyone make "a principled commitment to nonviolence" in order to participate in the civil rights movement. He explained:

> It is quite possible, and even probable, that American Negroes will adopt nonviolence as a means, an instrument for the achievement of specific and limited ends.... Certainly it would be wrong and even disastrous, to demand principled agreement on nonviolence as a precondition to nonviolent action. What is required is the spiritual determination of the people to be true to the

principle as it works *in this specific action.* This was the case in Montgomery, and it will continue to be the rule in further developments of our struggle.[37]

King readily admitted that there were relatively few participants in the movement absolutely committed to nonviolence as a way of life. King did not react negatively to those who accepted nonviolence only as a strategy because he felt that it could be the first step toward adopting it as a way of life. He was not a purist of the sort that Gandhi became during his later years; there was an element of pragmatism and realism in King's thought from the outset. Hence, he never refused offers of assistance from any quarter. During the Selma campaign, for example, those blacks who could not accept nonviolence, even as a method, were given instructions about ways they could assist, such as driving taxis, preparing food, or providing lodging. There were many participants in every campaign who accepted nonviolence as a method to achieve a specific objective who had no intention of subscribing to it as a way of life.

When King referred to nonviolence as "a method of action," he meant nonviolent resistance and nonviolent direct action. Nonviolent direct action included a variety of tactics, such as demonstrations, sit-ins, pray-ins, wade-ins, boycotts, and civil disobedience. One observer has called such tactics "creative disorder." King used various terms, such as tactic, policy, technique, and method, to describe nonviolent resistance. There seems to have been some conceptual confusion in King's mind at this point which is traceable to his failure to distinguish between *strategy* and *tactics* as these terms are used today in the literature on social change. It is important to comprehend the meaning and difference between strategy and tactics in order to understand the developments that took place in King's thought during the latter part of his life.

The terms "strategy" and "tactics" were used initially in military science. Strategy means the science of planning and directing large-scale military operations, specifically of maneuvering forces into the most advantageous position *prior* to the actual engagement of the enemy. Tactics means the science of arranging and maneuvering military forces *in action* — any skilled method to achieve an advantage. In the field of social change, strategy means the overall plan of action adopted, given various alternatives (e.g., violence or nonviolence), to pursue general goals or a specific objective. Tactics refers to the methods taken to implement the strategy. Strategy is in one sense analogous to policy-making — the choice of a plan to achieve social and political goals. A tactic is a specific action in a concrete situation.[38] To cite several examples: electoral politics is a strategy; a political campaign or a voter registration drive is a tactic. A coup d'etat by violence is a strategy; the assassination of key leaders of a government is a tactic. Nonviolent direct action is a strategy; an economic boycott is a tactic.

The point is that though King often referred to nonviolent resistance as a tactic or technique, it should properly be viewed as a strategy with many tactical manifestations. Some of the mistakes that King admitted, such as that he should have remained in jail in Montgomery and that the objectives of the Albany campaign were too vague, should be viewed as tactical errors within the general framework of the strategy of nonviolence. When King was severely criticized for his refusal to continue the second march from Selma to Montgomery in March 1965, he responded: "It was not that we didn't intend to go on to Montgomery, but that, in consideration of our commitment to nonviolent action, we knew we could not go under present conditions."[39] King was always ready to change his tactics if the situation seemed to warrant it. He knew that the appropriate tactic should be decided on the basis of the specific objective and should be commensurate with that objective. In other words, King was aware that flexibility in tactics is the best approach to constructive social action. Thus he always kept his options open, so that he could do the unexpected and thereby throw the opponent off balance.

Although there was some confusion in King's theory regarding the difference between strategy and tactics, it is obvious from his activity that he made a distinction in practice. This can be demonstrated by tracing the developments in King's attitudes toward the degree of "pressure" that would be required to achieve the goals of the civil rights movement. During the latter part of his career, especially the period following Birmingham and Selma, King began to express doubts about the viability of his tactics. A slow but perceptual shift took place in his thinking about the kind of countervailing power that would be required to "force" white society to share its economic and political power with the black population and other disinherited groups. There was a great deal of difference in King's attitude toward the efficacy of moral suasion after the Montgomery bus boycott and during the preparations for the Poor People's Campaign.

Prior to Birmingham and Selma, King was very optimistic about the efficacy of the strategy and tactics which had been used and the rapidity with which the goals of the civil rights movement would be achieved. During the Montgomery bus boycott, for example, he said, "The day of Senator Eastland is over." Shortly after the bus boycott had been successfully completed, he spoke confidently that the South would throw off its provincialism and racial segregation in the near future. However, King became less sure after Birmingham and Selma that his early assessment had been correct, because he began to realize, undoubtedly for the first time, that groups with power do not relinquish it without an all-out struggle.

When he realized the meaning of the so-called "white backlash" and that the poor blacks in the Northern ghettos had not gained anything appreciable from the civil rights legislation he had considered epoch-making, his doubts became more explicit. Thus by the time he published *Where Do We Go from Here: Chaos or Community?* in 1967, he had become keenly aware of the force of the arguments of the proponents of Black Power. While he disagreed with many aspects of the Black Power philosophy, he was forced to admit:

...it cannot be taken for granted that Negroes will adhere to nonviolence under any and all conditions. When there is rock-like intransigence of sophisticated manipulation that mocks the empty-handed petitioner, rage replaces reason. Nonviolence is a powerful demand for reason and justice. If it is rudely rebuked, it is not transformed into resignation and passivity.... The end of this road is clearly in sight. The cohesive, potentially explosive Negro community in the North has a short fuse and a long train of abuses. Those who argue that it is hazardous to give warnings, lest the expression of apprehension lead to violence, are in error. Violence has already been practiced too often, and always because remedies were postponed.[40]

The clearest statement of King's thinking about tactics during the last years of his life appears in his last book, *The Trumpet of Conscience*. In that book King outlined a position that clearly falls into the category of nonviolent sabotage — definitely a major step beyond "creative disorder." He argued that the tactics used earlier (i.e., demonstrations, sit-ins, boycotts, etc.) were no longer effective enough to produce structural changes in the system and that they should be supplanted by "massive civil disobedience." He explained:

Negroes must...fashion new tactics which do not count on government goodwill but serve, instead, to compel unwilling authorities to yield to the mandates of justice....

Nonviolent protest must now mature to a new level to correspond to heightened black impatience and stiffened white resistance. This higher level is mass civil disobedience. There must be more than a statement to the larger society; there must be a force that interrupts its functioning at some key point....

Mass civil disobedience as a new stage of struggle can transmute the deep rage of the ghetto into a constructive and creative force. *To dislocate the functioning of a city without destroying it* can be more effective than a riot because it can be longer-lasting, costly to the larger society, but not wantonly destructive. Finally, it is a device of social action that is more difficult for the government to quell by superior force.[41]

The evidence indicates that the Poor People's Campaign, if it had been carried out as King had envisaged it, would have been

the first step in the initiation of the new tactic of mass civil disobedience. The comments of Andrew J. Young, vice-president of
the Southern Christian Leadership Conference and one of King's
key lieutenants, about the plans for the Poor People's Campaign
are very revealing. Young said in an interview:

> Dr. King reached the conclusion that something needs to be done
> to really shock this country into its senses. To use a psychiatric
> metaphor, the country is sick and it needs a shock treatment....
>
> We have been reluctant to tie up a big city like we did in
> Birmingham. But we decided that we had better go ahead and
> dramatize these problems; and if it means tying up the country,
> then we just have to do it....
>
> The way Washington is, a few hundred people on each of
> those bridges would make it impossible to get in or out....It
> would mean that every day going back and forth you are thinking
> about three or four hours each way. That's another kind of civil
> disobedience.[42]

It is apparent that the kind of civil disobedience King had in
mind was quite different from the *classical Thoreauvian view
of civil disobedience. Thoreau refused to pay taxes as a protest
against the Mexican War, but he did not hope by his action to
force a change in national policy. While he encouraged others to
adopt similar protests, he did not attempt to mount any mass action against unjust practices. In contrast to Thoreau, King began
to advocate, just prior to his death, the use of mass civil disobedience to effect revolutionary (i.e., structural) changes within
the social system. Mass civil disobedience, as indicated, would include the disruption of the functioning of the social system — a
form of nonviolent sabotage.

It may seem strange to some readers to associate King with
nonviolent sabotage. For some it might even imply that King
had thereby abandoned the strategy of nonviolence. But this is
not the case if we keep in mind the distinction between strategy
and tactics and the alternative approaches to social change. In
Radicalism in America, Sidney Lens has pointed out:

> In the final analysis there are only three ways of effecting social
> change: through persuasion of the men who hold power in the

existing system, through a conspiratorial *coup d'etat*, or through the open mobilization of the people against the prevailing order. The first is the technique of liberals, the second of one type of anarchist, the third of most other radicals.[43]

King went to great lengths to disavow the charge of anarchism, though he endorsed civil disobedience. He criticized severely "urban riots" and "guerrilla romanticism," finding them both counterrevolutionary. During the Montgomery bus boycott and for several years thereafter, he described his activity as an attempt to persuade those in positions of power to see the justice of the black cause by appealing to their consciences to pass legislation that would abolish segregation and foster equal rights. This approach corresponds to Lens's description of liberalism — change through moral suasion, education, and legislation. King moved on in later campaigns (e.g., Birmingham, Selma) to creative disorder which in some instances included civil disobedience. The success of such campaigns depended upon "the open mobilization of the people." With the advocacy of nonviolent sabotage, King had obviously abandoned the strategy of liberalism and adopted the strategy of radicalism, "the open mobilization of the people against the prevailing system." However, he considered radicalism to be a nonviolent strategy; mass civil disobedience and nonviolent sabotage were conceived as tactics of nonviolence.

By employing the strategy of radicalism, King hoped to achieve a fundamental change in the priorities and structures of American society. Radicalism assumes that the basic institutions and structures of a social system must be changed drastically, not merely reformed. Whereas liberalism stresses persuasion, radicalism emphasizes power and coercion. For the liberal, cooperation and consensus are the important social processes; for the radical, conflict and confrontation are important. As King became more and more radical in his thinking, he placed more and more stress upon power, coercion, conflict, and confrontation. The shift in King's tactics indicates that he opted, in the final analysis, for what Reinhold Niebuhr had called "rational coercion" or "non-violent coercion." It is apparent, likewise, that Niebuhr had a greater influence upon King's thought at the point of tactics than anywhere else.

Although King changed his thinking about tactics, he never abandoned nonviolence as his strategy, and he never relinquished his personal faith in nonviolence as "a way of life." One of his last published articles contained the following passage:

> I'm just not going to kill anybody, whether it's in Vietnam or here. I'm not going to burn down any building. If non-violent protest fails this summer, I will continue to preach it and teach it, and we at Southern Christian Leadership Conference will still do this. I plan to stand by non-violence because I have found it to be a philosophy of life that regulates not only my dealings in the struggle for racial justice but also my dealings with people, with my own self. I will still be faithful to non-violence.[44]

Moreover, King did not abandon his belief that violence by black people in the United States would be a futile exercise leading to suicide. At the same time, he was prepared to employ all the tactics available that he considered consistent with the strategy of nonviolence, including nonviolent sabotage.

THE ACTUALIZATION OF THE BELOVED COMMUNITY

One of the questions that comes naturally to mind about ideal communities, like King's conception of the Beloved Community, is: can they be actualized within history? This question has been a subject of dispute in the Christian community throughout the twentieth century. The orthodox school of thought, without doubt the dominant school in the history of the Christian church, has held that the kingdom of God will be realized only by an act of God after the end of history. In this view, the kingdom of God is strictly an other-worldly phenomenon; its locus will be "above" or "beyond" historical existence. History is not a redemptive process because human beings do not possess the moral power to bring the millennial hope to fruition — that can be accomplished only by the grace and power of God. The dream of perpetual peace and unity will never be actualized within history because sin is a constant, not a variable within human nature. The avowal of ideals, no matter how lofty and noble, will not eliminate evil. In short, there will be a perennial tension between "the kingdoms of this world" and the kingdom of God until God intervenes at the end of history.

The school of thought at the opposite end of the spectrum from orthodoxy, Protestant liberalism, has held that the millennial hope will be actualized within history in the form of an ideal social order as sin is gradually overcome by education and science and as the inherent potentials of human nature are liberated. "The Kingdom of God," Rauschenbusch wrote, "is humanity organized according to the will of God.... [It] implies the progressive reign of love in human affairs."[45] Edgar S. Brightman observed:

> The world of shared values can reach such a level of cooperation that man is liberated from his selfishness and is empowered to give himself to his neighbor. On the level of cooperation the Kingdom of God is realized — where "all races and creeds can meet, learn, and respect each other in religious liberty."[46]

In this view, unlimited possibilities are open to humankind; human nature can be perfected, and human society can be redeemed.

Martin Luther King appropriated the themes of the social gospel of Rauschenbusch and the personalism of Brightman to express his views on the actualization of the Beloved Community. King had a firm and unshakable faith in the potentialities of human nature and the vitalities of history. Although his optimism was qualified to some extent by the realism of Reinhold Niebuhr, he insisted, nevertheless, that "there is within human nature an amazing potential for goodness,"[47] and he criticized Niebuhr for failing "to deal adequately with the relative perfection of the Christian life."[48] Just as the optimism of Rauschenbusch was due, not to the fact that he ignored human sin, but to his faith in the power of love, so with King. He maintained a confidence in humanity's ability to produce a better society, even an ideal society. King's position regarding the possibility of actualizing the Beloved Community within history was in accord with Rauschenbusch's view: God initiates the kingdom, but human effort will bring it to fruition.

King was confident that if those who were committed to nonviolence would continue to practice it, they could "bring into being a new nation where men will live together as brothers; a nation where all men will respect the dignity and worth of the human personality...."[49] King was able to make such an affirmation because he thought he discerned forces at work within American society that would assure integration. He remarked:

> Indeed it is the keystone of my faith in the future that we will someday achieve a thoroughly integrated society. I believe that before the turn of the century, if trends continue to move and develop as presently, we will have moved a long, long way toward such a society.[50]

However, King always hastened to add that the Beloved Community would not be produced automatically simply by the passage of time. He was acutely aware that the kingdom of God is "not yet" a reality and that there are still many obstacles to overcome. He had learned from Niebuhr that, given the nature of human nature and the demonic forces within history, the elimination of one evil often brings another to the surface. The actualization of the Beloved Community, therefore, will necessitate a persistent struggle against the demonic structures of injustice and an unswerving commitment to the ideals and values of the Judeo-Christian faith.

In his views on the possibility of actualizing the Beloved Community within history, King attempted to avoid what he called "a superficial optimism," on the one hand, and "a crippling pessimism," on the other hand. He knew that the elimination of

social problems is a slow process; at the same time, he was confident that social progress could be made through God's help and
human effort. He explained in a definitive passage:

> Although man's moral pilgrimage may never reach a destination
> point on earth, his never-ceasing strivings may bring him ever
> closer to the city of righteousness. And though the Kingdom of
> God may remain *not yet* as a universal reality in history, in the
> present it may exist in such isolated forms as in judgment, in
> personal devotion, and in some group life....
>
> Above all, we must be reminded anew that God is at work
> in his universe. He is not outside the world looking on with a
> sort of cold indifference.... As we struggle to defeat the forces of
> evil, the God of the universe struggles with us. Evil dies on the
> seashore, not merely because of man's endless struggle against it,
> but because of God's power to defeat it.[51]

Although Martin Luther King was acutely aware that the Beloved Community is "not yet," but in the future, perhaps even
the distant future, he believed that it would be actualized within
history, and he saw approximations of it already. Thus he worked
unceasingly for the realization of his dream, and he never lost
hope that "there will be a great camp meeting in the promised
land." His hope was rooted in his faith in the power of God to
achieve his purpose among humankind within history.

Notes

Introduction

1. Martin E. Marty and Dean G. Peerman, eds., *New Theology No. 6* (New York: The Macmillan Company, 1969), p. 184.

2. Daniel Day Williams, *The Spirit and the Forms of Love* (New York: Harper & Row, Publishers, 1968), p. 270.

3. Louis E. Lomax, *To Kill a Black Man* (Los Angeles: Holloway House Publishing Co., 1968), p. 93.

4. There are two versions of King's account of his "pilgrimage to non-violence": *Stride Toward Freedom* (New York: Harper & Row, Publishers, 1958), pp. 90–107 and *Strength to Love* (New York: Harper & Row, Publishers, 1963), pp. 135–142. The version in *Stride Toward Freedom* is the fullest and best statement.

5. Mathew Ahmann, ed., *Race: Challenge to Religion* (Chicago: Henry Regnery Co., 1963), pp. 164–165.

6. See Kenneth Cauthen, *The Impact of American Religious Liberalism* (New York: Harper & Row, Publishers, 1962), and Lloyd J. Averill, *American Theology in the Liberal Tradition* (Philadelphia: The Westminster Press, 1967).

7. L. D. Reddick, *Crusader Without Violence* (New York: Harper & Row, Publishers, 1959), chapter 6.

8. See Reddick, op. cit., chapter 5; Lerone Bennett Jr., *What Manner of Man* (Chicago: Johnson Publishing Company, 1964), chapter 1; David L. Lewis, *King, A Critical Biography* (New York: Praeger Publishers, 1970), chapter 1.

9. King, *Stride Toward Freedom*, p. 91. Copyright © 1958 by Martin Luther King Jr.

10. "Application to Crozer Theological Seminary" (February 18, 1948).

11. *Crusader* (April, 1957), p. 7.

12. See, for example, L. D. Reddick, *Crusader Without Violence*; Lerone Bennett Jr., *What Manner of Man*; David L. Lewis, *King, A Critical Biography*; and William Robert Miller, *Martin Luther King, Jr.: His Life, Martyrdom and Meaning for the World* (New York: Weybright & Talley, Inc., 1968).

13. Warren Carberg, *Bostonia* (April, 1959), p. 8.

14. Bennett, *What Manner of Man*, pp. 36–37, 39.

15. Miller, *Martin Luther King*, p. 17.

16. Ira G. Zepp Jr., "The Intellectual Sources of the Ethical Thought

157

of Martin Luther King, Jr." (Ph.D. dissertation, St. Mary's University and Seminary, Baltimore, Maryland, 1971).

17. See King, "My Trip to the Land of Gandhi," *Ebony* (July, 1959), pp. 84ff.

18. Quoted in Reddick, op. cit., p. 86.

19. Cf. two articles by Edwin E. Aubrey, president of Crozer from 1944 to 1949, for an excellent analysis of liberalism: "Our Liberal Heritage," *Chronicle,* vol. 7 (October, 1944), pp. 145–150 and "The Present Status of Liberalism," *Crozer Quarterly,* vol. 25 (January, 1948), pp. 1–11.

20. The text in the course was Robert H. Pfeiffer's *An Introduction to the Old Testament.*

21. The text in the course was Enslin's own *Christian Beginnings,* widely known and admired in New Testament circles.

22. Miller, op. cit., p. 17.

23. Albert Schweitzer, *The Quest of the Historical Jesus* (New York: The Macmillan Company, 1954), p. 398. (This volume was published in English in 1910.)

24. Cf. Enslin's review of a new edition of Schweitzer's *The Mystery of the Kingdom of God* in *Crozer Quarterly,* vol. 27 (July, 1950), p. 280.

25. King, *Stride Toward Freedom,* p. 84.

26. Reddick, op. cit., p. 79.

27. "Letter to Dr. George W. Davis" (December 1, 1953). The letter is in the possession of Davis's widow, Mrs. George W. Davis of Wilmington, Delaware.

Chapter One

1. See King's "Class Notes on 'Christian Mysticism'" (Boston Collection, Box IV). The library of Boston University in Boston, Massachusetts, contains a large collection of unpublished material by King, especially for the years 1954–1964. Some of it has been catalogued and some of it has not. Henceforth, items from this material will be referred to as the Boston Collection, with location whenever possible. Quoted by permission of Joan Daves.

2. King, *Strength to Love* (New York: Harper & Row, Publishers, 1963), p. 137.

3. L. D. Reddick, *Crusader Without Violence* (New York: Harper & Row, Publishers, 1959), p. 79.

4. "Permanent Record of Martin Luther King, Jr." (Crozer Theological Seminary, December 15, 1950).

5. *The Bulletin of Crozer Theological Seminary,* vol. 41 (January, 1949), p. 25.

6. Ibid., p. 26.

7. New York: Charles Scribner's Sons, 1909.

8. New York: Charles Scribner's Sons, 1906.

9. William Newton Clarke, *An Outline of Christian Theology* (New York: Charles Scribner's Sons, 1909), p. 1.

10. Ibid., p. 20.

11. "Letter to Dr. George W. Davis."

12. Ibid.

13. Cf. "In Praise of Liberalism," *Theology Today*, vol. 4, no. 4 (January, 1948), pp. 491–492.

14. George W. Davis, "Liberalism and a Theology of Depth," *Crozer Quarterly*, vol. 28 (July, 1951), p. 201.

15. King, *Where Do We Go From Here: Chaos or Community?* (New York: Harper & Row, Publishers, 1967), p. 1. Copyright © 1967 by Martin Luther King Jr.

16. George W. Davis, "God and History," *Crozer Quarterly*, vol. 20 (January, 1943), p. 19.

17. King, *Strength to Love*, p. 64. Copyright © 1963 by Martin Luther King Jr.

18. King, *Stride Toward Freedom* (New York: Harper & Row, Publishers, 1958), p. 160.

19. Davis, "God and History," p. 25.

20. King, *Stride Toward Freedom*, p. 100.

21. Davis, "God and History," pp. 27–28.

22. Ibid., p. 31.

23. Ibid.

24. Davis, "Liberalism and a Theology of Depth," p. 205.

25. George W. Davis, "The Ethical Basis of Christian Salvation," *Crozer Quarterly*, vol. 16 (July, 1939), p. 181.

26. King, *Strength to Love*, p. 135.

27. Davis, "Liberalism and a Theology of Depth," p. 193.

28. Ibid., p. 195.

29. Ibid., p. 198.

30. "Letter to Dr. George W. Davis."

31. "Report of Seminar on 'Systematic Theology'" for L. Harold DeWolf during 1951–1952 (Boston Collection).

Chapter Two

1. King, *Strength to Love* (New York: Harper & Row, Publishers, 1963), p. 138.

2. H. Richard Niebuhr, *The Kingdom of God in America* (New York: Harper & Row, Publishers, Harper Torchbook, 1959), p. 162.

3. Cf. D. R. Sharpe, *Walter Rauschenbusch* (New York: The Macmillan Company, 1942).

4. Robert T. Handy, ed., *The Social Gospel in America, 1870–1920* (New York: Oxford University Press, 1966), p. 255.

5. Cf. H. Shelton Smith, *Changing Conceptions of Original Sin* (New York: Charles Scribner's Sons, 1955), chapter 9; Richard Dickinson, "Rauschenbusch and Niebuhr: Brothers Under the Skin?" *Religion in Life,* vol. 27 (Spring, 1958), pp. 163–171; Walter Rauschenbusch, *The Righteousness of the Kingdom,* edited and introduced by Max L. Stackhouse (Nashville: Abingdon Press, 1968), Part I.

6. Walter Rauschenbusch, *Christianity and the Social Crisis* (New York: Harper & Row, Publishers, 1964), p. 98.

7. Ibid., p. 361.

8. Ibid., p. 176.

9. Walter Rauschenbusch, *A Theology for the Social Gospel* (New York: The Macmillan Company, 1917), p. 194.

10. Rauschenbusch, *Christianity and the Social Crisis,* p. 338.

11. King, "Statement to Judge Loe" (Boston Collection), p. 1.

12. King, *Stride Toward Freedom* (New York: Harper & Row, Publishers, 1958), p. 40.

13. Rauschenbusch, *Christianity and the Social Crisis,* p. 342.

14. Rauschenbusch, *A Theology for the Social Gospel,* p. 75.

15. Rauschenbusch, *Christianity and the Social Crisis,* p. 349.

16. King, *Stride Toward Freedom,* p. 205.

17. King, *Where Do We Go from Here: Chaos or Community?* (New York: Harper & Row, Publishers, 1967), p. 96.

18. King, *Strength to Love,* p. 98.

19. King, *Why We Can't Wait* (New York: Harper & Row, Publishers, 1963), p. 96. Copyright © 1963 by Martin Luther King Jr.

20. King, *Strength to Love,* p. 97.

21. King, *Why We Can't Wait,* p. 95.

22. King, *Stride Toward Freedom,* pp. 116–117.

23. Ibid., p. 117.

24. Rauschenbusch, *A Theology for the Social Gospel,* p. 131.

25. Rauschenbusch, *Christianity and the Social Crisis,* p. xiii.

26. Ibid., p. 65.

27. Rauschenbusch, *A Theology for the Social Gospel,* pp. 142, 155.

28. Ibid., p. 142.

29. Rauschenbusch, *Christianity and the Social Crisis,* p. 420.

30. King, *Stride Toward Freedom,* p. 91.

Chapter Three

1. King, *Stride Toward Freedom* (New York: Harper & Row, Publishers, 1958), p. 95.

2. *Bulletin of Crozer Theological Seminary*, vol. 43 (January, 1951), p. 29. Hereinafter cited as *Bulletin*.

3. "A Realistic Look at the Question of Progress in the Area of Race Relations" (Boston Collection), p. 7.

4. King, *Stride Toward Freedom*, p. 85.

5. Ibid., p. 97.

6. Ibid., p. 85.

7. C. F. Andrews, *Mahatma Gandhi's Ideas* (New York: The Macmillan Company, 1930), p. 60.

8. *Ahimsa* is the cardinal tenet of Jainism, a Hindu reform movement dating back to the sixth century B.C. It was very prominent in Gandhi's home state of Gujarat, and Gandhi's mother had been influenced significantly by Jainism.

9. Erik H. Erikson, *Gandhi's Truth* (New York: W. W. Norton, Inc., 1969), p. 412.

10. M. K. Gandhi, *Non-Violent Resistance* (New York: Schocken Books, Inc., 1968), p. 161.

11. Quoted in Creighton Lacy, *The Conscience of India* (New York: Holt, Rinehart & Winston, Inc., 1965), p. 147.

12. Gandhi, *Non-Violent Resistance*, p. 15.

13. Joan V. Bondurant, *Conquest of Violence: The Gandhian Philosophy of Conflict* (Princeton: Princeton University Press, 1958), p. 112.

14. Gandhi, *Non-Violent Resistance*, p. 165.

15. Cf. King, *Stride Toward Freedom*, p. 220: "If he [the Black] has to go to jail for the cause of freedom, let him enter it in the fashion Gandhi urged his countrymen, 'as the bridegroom enters the bride's chamber' — that is, with a little trepidation but with a great expectation."

16. Henry David Thoreau, "On the Duty of Civil Disobedience," *Walden* (New York: New American Library, 1962, A Signet Classic), p. 230.

17. Gandhi, *Non-Violent Resistance*, p. 175.

18. Reinhold Niebuhr, *Moral Man and Immoral Society* (New York: Charles Scribner's Sons, 1952), p. 172.

19. Quoted in Louis Fischer, *The Life of Mahatma Gandhi* (New York: Harper & Row, Publishers, 1950), p. 103.

20. Ibid.

21. King, *Stride Toward Freedom*, p. 212.

22. *Christianity and Society* (Spring, 1956), p. 3.

23. King, "The Ethical Demands of Integration," *Religion and Labor* (May, 1963), p. 9.

24. *New South*, vol. 16 (December, 1961), pp. 3–11.

25. King, *Stride Toward Freedom*, p. 102.

26. Ibid. See Gandhi, *Non-Violent Resistance*, p. 132: "I do believe that where there is only a choice between cowardice and violence, I would advise violence."

27. King, *Stride Toward Freedom*, p. 102.

28. Ibid.

29. Ibid, p. 217.

30. Richard B. Gregg, *The Power of Non-Violence*, 2nd rev. ed. (New York: Schocken Books, Inc., 1959).

31. Ibid., p. 44.

32. Ibid., p. 45.

33. King, *Why We Can't Wait* (New York: Harper & Row, Publishers, 1963), pp. 107–108.

34. "Interview with Martin Luther King," *Playboy* (January, 1965), p. 120.

35. King, *Stride Toward Freedom*, p. 102.

36. Ibid., p. 103.

37. Ibid.

38. Ibid.

39. Ibid., p. 106.

40. Ibid., p. 107.

41. King, *Where Do We Go from Here: Chaos or Community?* (New York: Harper & Row, Publishers, 1967), p. 77.

42. King, *Stride Toward Freedom*, p. 103.

43. *Bulletin*, vol. 43 (January, 1951), p. 31.

44. Compare King's description of *eros* and *agape* in *Stride Toward Freedom* (p. 104) with Anders Nygren's description of *agape*, in *Agape and Eros*, trans., Philip S. Watson (Philadelphia: The Westminster Press, 1953), pp. 75–81.

45. King, *Stride Toward Freedom*, p. 104.

46. Nygren, op. cit., pp. 75–81.

47. King, *Stride Toward Freedom*, pp. 104–105.

48. Ibid., p. 105.

49. Paul Ramsey, *Basic Christian Ethics* (New York: Charles Scribner's Sons, 1950), pp. 94, 95.

50. King, *Stride Toward Freedom*, p. 105.

51. Ramsey, op. cit., p. 238.

52. King, *Stride Toward Freedom*, pp. 105, 106.

53. Ibid., p. 105.

54. Nygren, op. cit., p. 78.

55. Ramsey, op. cit., pp. 2, 3, 13.

56. Ibid., p. 94.

57. King, "The Ethical Demands of Integration," p. 4.

58. Albert C. Knudson, *The Principles of Christian Ethics* (Nashville: Abingdon Press, 1943), p. 137.

59. Ibid., p. 64.

60. Ibid., p. 65.

61. Ibid., p. 77.

62. See "Transcript" from University of Pennsylvania and "Notes and Exams on Kant" (Boston Collection, Box XIV).

63. Edward Long, *Conscience and Compromise* (Philadelphia: The Westminster Press, 1954), p. 28.

64. King, *Stride Toward Freedom*, p. 99.

65. Ibid., p. 117.

66. King, *Why We Can't Wait*, p. 85. King was quite familiar with Aristotle and Thomism from his many courses on philosophy, theology, and ethics. For example, one of his term papers for an ethics course at Crozer, to be described below, was entitled "The Political Philosophy of Jacques Maritain."

67. King, *Stride Toward Freedom*, p. 149.

68. King, *Why We Can't Wait*, p. 19.

Chapter Four

1. King, *Stride Toward Freedom* (New York: Harper & Row, Publishers, 1958), p. 97.

2. Cf. *The Bulletin of Crozer Theological Seminary*, vol. 43 (January, 1951), p. 30.

3. Cf. *Stride Toward Freedom*, p. 98; *Strength to Love* (New York: Harper & Row, Publishers, 1963), p. 91; *Why We Can't Wait* (New York: Harper & Row, Publishers, 1963), p. 82; *Where Do We Go from Here: Chaos or Community?* (New York: Harper & Row, Publishers, 1967), p. 143; "Interview with Martin Luther King," *Playboy* (January, 1965), p. 128.

4. King, *Strength to Love*, p. 135.

5. King, *Stride Toward Freedom*, p. 97.

6. *Christianity and Crisis*, vol. 31, no. 7 (May 3, 1971), p. 80. Copyright © 1971 by Christianity and Crisis, Inc.

7. King, *Stride Toward Freedom*, p. 99.

8. Ibid.

9. Reinhold Niebuhr, *The Nature and Destiny of Man*, one vol. ed. (New York: Charles Scribner's Sons, 1947), vol. 1, pp. 150ff.

10. Ibid., p. 13.

11. Ibid., p. 162.

12. Ibid., p. 150.

13. Reinhold Niebuhr, *The Children of Light and the Children of Darkness* (New York: Charles Scribner's Sons, 1944), p. xi (words in brackets added).

14. King, *Strength to Love*, p. 136.

15. Ibid., p. 88.

16. Ibid.

17. Ibid., p. 90.

18. Ibid., pp. 133–134.

19. Ibid., p. 91.

20. Reinhold Niebuhr, *Moral Man and Immoral Society* (New York: Charles Scribner's Sons, 1952), p. 44.

21. Ibid., p. 117.

22. King, *Strength to Love*, p. 136.

23. King, *Stride Toward Freedom*, p. 119.

24. King, "Love, Law and Civil Disobedience," *New South*, vol. 16 (December, 1961), p. 6.

25. Ibid.

26. Ibid., p. 7.

27. King, "Reinhold Niebuhr's Ethical Dualism" (A term paper written for L. Harold DeWolf: Boston Collection), p. 14.

28. Ibid.

29. King, *Stride Toward Freedom*, p. 99.

30. Ibid.

31. Niebuhr, *Moral Man and Immoral Society*, p. 234.

32. Niebuhr, *The Nature and Destiny of Man*, vol. 2, p. 256.

33. Reinhold Niebuhr, *An Interpretation of Christian Ethics* (New York: Harper & Row, Publishers, 1935, Meridian Books, 1956), chapter 4.

34. *Love and Justice, Selections from the Shorter Writings of Reinhold Niebuhr*, edited by D. B. Robertson (New York: The World Publishing Company, Meridian Books, 1967), p. 33.

35. Reinhold Niebuhr, *Christianity and Power Politics* (New York: Charles Scribner's Sons, 1946), pp. 26–27.

36. King, "The Un-Christian Christian," *Ebony*, vol. 20 (August, 1965), p. 79.

37. King, *Why We Can't Wait*, p. 123.

38. "Interview with Martin Luther King" *Playboy* (January, 1965), p. 128.

39. King, "Equality Now," *The Nation* (February 4, 1961), p. 93.

40. King, *Where Do We Go from Here . . . ?* pp. 128–129 (italics added).

41. King, "The Right to Vote," *New York Times Magazine* (March 14, 1965), p. 95.

42. King, *Where Do We Go from Here . . . ?* p. 129. See King, "Honoring Dr. Du Bois," *Freedomways* (Spring, 1968), pp. 104ff.

43. Ibid., pp. 89–90.

44. Ibid., p. 90.

45. King, "The Ethical Demands of Integration," *Religion and Labor* (May, 1963), p. 4.

46. King, "The American Dream," *Negro History Bulletin*, vol. 31, no. 5 (May 1968), p. 14.

47. King, *Strength to Love*, p. 22. See Reinhold Niebuhr, "The Montgomery Savagery," *Christianity and Crisis* (June 12, 1961), p. 103: "The whip of the law cannot change the heart. But thank God it can restrain the heartless until they change their mind and heart."

48. King, *Where Do We Go from Here...?* p. 90.

49. Ibid., p. 37. This passage reflects the influence of Paul Tillich's *Love, Power and Justice* (New York: Oxford University Press, 1954).

50. See James E. Sellers, "Love, Justice and the Non-Violent Movement," *Theology Today*, vol. 18, no. 4 (January, 1962), pp. 427 and 428: "In King's reflections on the nonviolent movement, justice seems to stand as the highest goal of a Christian society, with love, accordingly, subordinated as the method or device by which that goal is to be attained....

"Clearly...love does not always occupy the pinnacle, the position of the *summum bonum*. Instead, justice...more nearly forms the content of this ideal." Our analysis of King's views on the relationship between love and justice shows that Sellers' position cannot be substantiated. It is clear beyond a shadow of doubt that love *is* the *summum bonum* in King's thought. It is true, to be sure, that King referred to love as a method; it *is* the heart of the strategy of nonviolence and nonviolent direct action. But King also conceived of love as the absolute norm of human behavior (i.e., "a way of life") and the ultimate goal of human society (i.e., the "Beloved Community").

51. Reinhold Niebuhr in A. Dudley Ward, ed., *The Goals of Economic Life* (New York: Harper & Row, Publishers, 1956), p. 451.

52. Niebuhr, *Christianity and Power Politics*, p. 8.

53. Niebuhr, *Moral Man and Immoral Society*, p. 242.

54. Ibid., p. 240.

55. King, *Stride Toward Freedom*, p. 98.

56. Cf. Niebuhr, *Moral Man and Immoral Society*, p. 241–256.

57. See Niebuhr, *The Nature and Destiny of Man*, vol. 2, p. 261.

58. Niebuhr, *Moral Man and Immoral Society*, p. 252.

59. Ibid., pp. 252, 253, 254.

60. However, Niebuhr denounced the Vietnam war, and he commended King for his stand against the war. See Niebuhr's foreword to a pamphlet, published by Clergy and Laymen Concerned About Vietnam, of King's address in Los Angeles (February 25, 1967), entitled "The Casualties of the War in Viet Nam."

61. Reinhold Niebuhr, *Beyond Tragedy* (New York: Charles Scribner's Sons, 1946), p. 187.

62. Niebuhr, *An Interpretation of Christian Ethics*, p. 169.

63. King, *Stride Toward Freedom*, p. 99.

64. A close analysis of King's speeches against the war in Vietnam reveals that most of his arguments were pragmatic instead of moral.

65. King, "Who Is Their God?" *The Nation* (October 13, 1962), p. 210.

66. Robertson, *Love and Justice*, p. 20.

67. See Note #60 above.

68. *Christianity and Society*, vol. 21 (Spring, 1956), p. 3.

69. "The Casualties of the War in Viet Nam," p. 3.

70. "Letter to Ira G. Zepp, Jr." (September 22, 1969).

Chapter Five

1. *Crozer Quarterly*, vol. 20 (January, 1943), p. 62.

2. *Bostonia* (Spring, 1957), p. 7.

3. King, *Stride Toward Freedom* (New York: Harper & Row, Publishers, 1958), p. 100.

4. Albert C. Knudson, *The Philosophy of Personalism* (New York: Abingdon Press, 1927), p. 237.

5. Edgar S. Brightman, *Nature and Values* (Nashville: Abingdon Press, 1945), p. 113.

6. Edgar S. Brightman, *An Introduction to Philosophy*, Revised by Robert N. Beck (New York: Holt, Rinehart & Winston, Inc., 1963), p. 330. (This book was published for the first time in 1925 and revised by Brightman in 1951.)

7. Knudson, *The Philosophy of Personalism*, p. 76.

8. Brightman, *Nature and Values*, p. 60.

9. Ibid., p. 115.

10. Ibid., p. 140.

11. Ibid., pp. 138–139.

12. King, *Strength to Love* (New York: Harper & Row, Publishers, 1963), p. 75.

13. Cf. Brightman, "The Essence of Christianity," *Crozer Quarterly*, vol. 18 (April, 1941), p. 119: "It is safe to say that no one at any stage of Christian development has ever read the story of Good Friday and of Easter without seeing in it the drama of faith in the spiritual value of sacrifice. *Out of voluntary submission to undeserved suffering come resurrection and redemption.* Here is a universal faith essential to all Christians everywhere" (italics added). This article was required reading in many of Davis's classes.

14. Knudson, *The Philosophy of Personalism*, p. 254.

15. King, *Stride Toward Freedom*, p. 100.

16. Brightman, *Nature and Values*, p. 150.

17. Edgar S. Brightman, *Moral Laws* (New York: Abingdon Press, 1933), p. 242.

18. Brightman, *Nature and Values*, p. 164.

19. King, *Where Do We Go from Here: Chaos or Community?* (New York: Harper & Row, Publishers, 1967), p. 97.

20. Ibid.

21. King, "A Realistic Look at the Question of Progress in the Area of Race Relations" (Boston Collection), p. 3.

22. King, "The Ethical Demands of Integration," *Religion and Labor* (May, 1963), p. 7.

23. Brightman, *Nature and Values*, p. 161.

24. King, *Where Do We Go from Here...?* p. 99.

25. Ibid., p. 97.

26. Ibid., pp. 99–100.

27. Ibid., p. 97.

28. Ibid.

29. Ibid., p. 180.

30. Brightman, *Nature and Values*, p. 140.

31. Edgar S. Brightman, *A Philosophy of Religion* (New York: Prentice Hall, Inc., 1940), p. 226.

32. Brightman, *An Introduction to Philosophy*, p. 279.

33. Brightman, *Nature and Values*, p. 72.

34. Cf. L. Harold DeWolf, *A Theology of the Living Church*, 2nd rev. ed. (New York: Harper & Row, Publishers, 1968), pp. 134–137. (This book was first published in 1953, and King mentioned it in his letter to Davis noted earlier.)

35. King, "A Comparison of the Conceptions of God in the Thinking of Paul Tillich and Henry Nelson Wieman" (Ph.D. dissertation, Boston University, 1955), p. 269.

36. King, *Strength to Love*, p. 141.

37. King, "A Comparison of the Conceptions of God..." p. 270.

38. King, *Strength to Love*, p. 94.

39. Ibid., pp. 141–142.

40. Brightman, *Moral Laws*, p. 286.

41. Ibid., p. 264.

42. Knudson, *The Philosophy of Personalism*, p. 155.

43. King, *Strength to Love*, pp. 104–105.

44. King, *Where Do We Go from Here...?* p. 180.

45. King, *Stride Toward Freedom*, pp. 69–70.

46. King, *Strength to Love*, p. 63. See the excellent article by James H. Smylie, "On Jesus, Pharaohs, and the Chosen People: Martin Luther King as Biblical Interpreter and Humanist," *Interpretation*, vol. 24 (January, 1970), pp. 74–91. Herein King's understanding of the Exodus event is examined in some detail.

47. Ibid., p. 104.

48. King, *Stride Toward Freedom*, p. 107.

49. King, "Love, Law and Civil Disobedience," *New South*, vol. 16 (December, 1961), p. 10.

50. Albert C. Knudson, *The Principles of Christian Ethics* (New York: Abingdon Press, 1943), p. 214.

51. Brightman, *Introduction to Philosophy*, p. 353.

52. Knudson, *The Principles of Christian Ethics*, p. 118.

53. Brightman, *Nature and Values*, p. 117.

54. King, *Stride Toward Freedom*, p. 100.

55. Bertocci revealed this information in a personal interview with one of the authors (Zepp). The main text was J. B. Baillie's translation of Hegel's *Phenomenology of Mind*, 2nd ed. (New York: Allen and Unwin, 1931). For a discussion of the relationship between master and slave, see pp. 234–240.

56. King, *Stride Toward Freedom*, pp. 100–101.

57. King, *Strength to Love*, p. 1.

58. Ibid., p. 99.

59. Ibid., p. 136.

60. King, *Stride Toward Freedom*, p. 213.

61. King, *Strength to Love*, p. 88.

62. King, *Stride Toward Freedom*, p. 101.

63. King, "Facing the Challenge of a New Age," *Phylon*, vol. 18 (April, 1957), p. 25.

64. King, *Stride Toward Freedom*, p. 44.

65. Ibid., pp. 196–197.

66. King, "A Realistic Look at the Question of Progress in the Area of Race Relations" (Boston Collection), p. 2.

Chapter Six

1. King, "The Ethical Demands of Integration," *Religion and Labor* (May, 1963), p. 7.

2. King, "Facing the Challenge of a New Age," *Phylon*, vol. 18 (April, 1957), p. 30.

3. King, *The Trumpet of Conscience* (New York: Harper & Row, Publishers, 1967), p. 68. Copyright © 1967 by Martin Luther King Jr.

4. Francis L. Broderick and August Meier, eds., *Negro Protest Thought in the Twentieth Century* (New York: The Bobbs-Merrill Co., Inc., 1965), p. 272.

5. King, "The Ethical Demands of Integration," p. 4.

6. Ibid.

7. King, *Why We Can't Wait* (New York: Harper & Row, Publishers, 1963), p. 168.

8. *Negro History Bulletin*, vol. 31, no. 5 (May, 1968), p. 22.

9. King, *Where Do We Go from Here: Chaos or Community?* (New York: Harper & Row, Publishers, 1967), p. 181.

10. Ibid., p. 9.

11. Ibid., p. 181.

12. King, "Honoring Dr. Du Bois," *Freedomways*, vol. 8, no. 2 (Spring, 1968), pp. 110–111.

13. King, *The Trumpet of Conscience*, p. 56.

14. King, *Strength to Love* (New York: Harper & Row, Publishers, 1963), p. 137.

15. King, *Stride Toward Freedom* (New York: Harper & Row, Publishers, 1958), p. 92.

16. Ibid., 95.

17. King, *Strength to Love*, pp. 98–99.

18. Harvey Cox, *On Not Leaving It to the Snake* (New York: The Macmillan Company, 1967), p. 133.

19. King, "The Rising Tide of Racial Consciousness," *The YWCA Magazine* (December, 1960), p. 3. For the full text of "I Have a Dream," see *Negro History Bulletin*, vol. 31 (May, 1968), or Bradford Chambers, ed., *Chronicles of Black Protest* (New York: Mentor Books, 1968), pp. 185–186.

20. Conversation with Ira G. Zepp Jr. (January 23, 1971).

21. *Negro History Bulletin*, vol. 31, no. 5 (May, 1968), p. 17.

22. Ibid., p. 10.

23. Ibid., p. 21.

24. King, "A Testament of Hope," *Playboy* (January, 1969), p. 234.

25. John Dixon Elder, "Martin Luther King and American Civil Religion," *Harvard Divinity School Bulletin*, vol. 1, no. 3 (Spring, 1968), p. 17.

26. Ibid., p. 18.

27. See Waldo Beach, *Christian Community and American Society* (Philadelphia: The Westminster Press, 1969), pp. 149–159.

28. James Cone, *Black Theology and Black Power* (New York: The Seabury Press, Inc., 1969), p. 108.

29. "What a Christian Should Think About the Kingdom of God" (Boston Collection), p. 2.

30. Reinhold Niebuhr, *Moral Man and Immoral Society* (New York: Charles Scribner's Sons, 1952), pp. 60–61.

31. King, *Strength to Love*, p. 19.

32. See King, *Trumpet of Conscience*, pp. 77–78. Herein King paraphrases his favorite passages from the prophets (Amos 5:24; Micah 6:8; Isaiah 2:4 and 40:3–5).

33. King, *Stride Toward Freedom*, p. 104.

34. Ibid., pp. 105–106.

35. Harvey Cox, *God's Revolution and Man's Responsibility* (Valley Forge: Judson Press, 1965), pp. 58–70.

36. Kenneth B. Clark, ed., "Martin Luther King Talks with Kenneth B. Clark," *The Negro Protest* (Boston: Beacon Press, 1963), pp. 39–40.

37. From an untitled manuscript in the Boston Collection, pp. 6–7. The manuscript was apparently written for *Challenge*, but it was never published in this form.

38. See Dieter T. Hessel, *A Social Action Primer* (Philadelphia: The Westminster Press, 1972), chapters 5 and 6.

39. King, "Behind the Selma March," *Saturday Review* (April 3, 1965), p. 57.

40. King, *Where Do We Go from Here...?*, p. 21.

41. King, *Trumpet of Conscience*, pp. 14, 15 (italics added) and King, "A New Sense of Direction," *Worldview*, vol. 15, no. 4 (April, 1972), pp. 5–12.

42. *Christianity and Crisis*, vol. 27, no. 24 (January 22, 1968), pp. 327–328. Copyright © 1968 by Christianity and Crisis, Inc.

43. Sidney Lens, *Radicalism in America* (New York: Thomas Y. Crowell Company, 1966), p. 357.

44. King, "Showdown for Nonviolence," *Look* (April 16, 1968), p. 25.

45. Rauschenbusch, *A Theology for the Social Gospel* (New York: The Macmillan Company, 1917), p. 142.

46. Edgar S. Brightman, *Nature and Values* (Nashville: Abingdon Press, 1945), p. 165.

47. King, "Love, Law and Civil Disobedience," *New South*, vol. 16 (December, 1961), p. 6.

48. King, "Reinhold Niebuhr's Ethical Dualism" (Boston Collection), p. 14.

49. King, "A View of the Dawn," *Interracial Review*, vol. 30, no. 5 (May, 1957), p. 85.

50. "An Interview with Martin Luther King," *Playboy* (January, 1965), p. 128.

51. King, *Strength to Love*, p. 64.

Selected Bibliography

I. BOOKS by *Martin Luther King Jr.*

King, Martin Luther, Jr. "A Comparison of the Conceptions of God in the Thinking of Paul Tillich and Henry Nelson Wieman" (unpublished Ph.D. dissertation, Boston University, 1955).

————, *Stride Toward Freedom: The Montgomery Story.* New York: Harper & Row, Publishers, 1958.

————, *The Measure of a Man.* Philadelphia: Christian Education Press, 1959.

————, *Strength to Love.* New York: Harper & Row, Publishers, 1963.

————, *Why We Can't Wait.* New York: Harper & Row, Publishers, 1963.

————, *Where Do We Go from Here: Chaos or Community?* New York: Harper & Row, Publishers, 1967.

————, *The Trumpet of Conscience.* New York: Harper & Row, Publishers, 1967.

————, *The Trumpet of Conscience* (Foreword by Coretta Scott King). New York: Harper & Row, Publishers, 1968.

————, *The Measure of a Man* (biographical sketch by Truman Douglas). Boston: Pilgrim Press, 1968.

————, *A Martin Luther King Treasury,* ed., Alfred E. Cain, The Negro Heritage Library. Yonkers: Educational Heritage, Inc., 1964.

II. CHAPTERS (in books) by *Martin Luther King Jr.*

King, Martin Luther, Jr. "Nonviolence and Racial Justice," Harold Fey and Margaret Frakes, eds., *The Christian Century Reader.* New York: Association Press, 1957.

————, "The Future of Integration," H. John Heinz, ed., *Crisis in Modern America.* New Haven: Yale University Press, 1959.

————, "Foreword," Richard Gregg, *The Power of Nonviolence.* New York: Schocken Books, Inc., 1959 (second edition).

————, "Where Do We Go from Here?" Harry K. Girvetz, ed., *Contemporary Moral Issues.* Belmont, Calif.: Wadsworth Publishing Co., Inc., 1963.

————, "A Challenge to the Churches and Synagogues," Mathew Ahmann, ed., *Race: Challenge to Religion.* Chicago: Henry Regnery Co., 1963.

————, "Martin Luther King Talks with Kenneth B. Clark," Kenneth B. Clark, ed., *The Negro Protest*. Boston: Beacon Press, 1963.

————, "Introduction," William Bradford Huie, *Three Lives for Mississippi*. New York: The New American Library, Inc., 1964.

————, "Introduction," Edward T. Clayton, *The Negro Politician: His Success and Failure*. Chicago: Johnson Publishing Co.–Book Division, 1964.

————, "Pilgrimage to Nonviolence," Staughton Lynd, ed., *Nonviolence in America: A Documentary History*. New York: The Bobbs-Merrill Co., Inc., 1966.

————, "Letter from the Birmingham Jail," Staughton Lynd, ed., *Nonviolence in America: A Documentary History*. New York: The Bobbs-Merrill Co., Inc., 1966.

————, "The Un-Christian Christian," Editors of Ebony, *The White Problem in America*. Chicago: Johnson Publishing Co.–Book Division, 1966.

————, "I Have a Dream," John Hope Franklin and Isidore Starr, eds., *The Negro in Twentieth Century America*. New York: Vintage Books (Random House, Inc.), 1967.

————, "Declaration of Independence from the War in Viet Nam," Michael Hamilton, ed., *The Viet Nam War: Christian Perspectives*. Grand Rapids: Wm. B. Eerdmans Publishing Co., 1967.

————, "I Have a Dream," Bradford Chambers, ed., *Chronicles of Black Protest*. New York: The New American Library, Inc., 1968.

————, "The Day of Days, December 5," Bradford Chambers, ed., *Chronicles of Black Protest*. New York: The New American Library Inc., 1968.

————, "Call to Conscience," Lester Thonssen, ed., *Representative American Speeches, 1963–1964*. New York: H. W. Williams, 1964.

III. ARTICLES by *Martin Luther King Jr.*

King, Martin Luther Jr., "Our Struggle," *Liberation* (April, 1956), pp. 1ff.

————, "Walk for Freedom," *Fellowship*, vol. 22 (May, 1956), pp. 5ff.

————, "We Are Still Walking," *Liberation* (December, 1956), pp. 6ff.

————, "Facing the Challenge of a New Age," *Phylon*, vol. 18 (Spring, 1957), pp. 25ff.

————, "Nonviolence and Racial Justice," *The Christian Century*, vol. 74 (February 6, 1957), pp. 165–167.

————, "The Most Durable Power," *The Christian Century*, vol. 74 (June 5, 1957), p. 708.

————, "A View of the Dawn," *Interracial Review* (May, 1957), pp. 82ff.

————, "Out of the Long Night of Segregation," *Advance*, vol. 150 (February 28, 1958), pp. 14ff.

———, "Out of Segregation's Long Night: An Interpretation of a Racial Crisis," *The Churchman*, vol. 172 (February, 1958), pp. 7ff.

———, "The Current Crisis in Race Relations," *New South* (March, 1958), pp. 8ff.

———, "Who Speaks for the South?" *Liberation* (March, 1958), pp. 13ff.

———, "The Ethics of Love," *Religious Digest*, (April, 1958), pp. 1ff.

———, "The Power of Nonviolence," *The Intercollegian* (May, 1958), pp. 8ff.

———, "An Experiment in Love," *Jubilee* (September, 1958), pp. 11ff.

———, "The Church and the Race Crisis," *The Christian Century*, vol. 75 (October 8, 1958), pp. 1140–1141.

———, "My Trip to the Land of Gandhi," *Ebony* (July, 1959), pp. 84ff.

———, "The Social Organization of Nonviolence," *Liberation* (October, 1959), pp. 5ff.

———, "Pilgrimage to Nonviolence," *The Christian Century*, vol. 77 (April 13, 1960), pp. 439–441.

———, "Suffering and Faith," *The Christian Century*, vol. 77 (April 27, 1960), p. 510.

———, "The Burning Truth in the South," *The Progressive*, vol. 24 (May, 1960), pp. 8ff.

———, "The Rising Tide of Racial Consciousness," *The YWCA Magazine* (December, 1960), pp. 12ff.

———, "Equality Now: The President Has the Power," *The Nation*, vol. 192 (February 4, 1961), pp. 91–95.

———, "The Time for Freedom Has Come," *The New York Times Magazine* (September 10, 1961), p. 25.

———, "Love, Law, and Civil Disobedience," *New South* (December, 1961), pp. 3ff.

———, "Fumbling on the New Frontier," *The Nation*, vol. 194 (March 3, 1962), pp. 190–193.

———, "The Case Against Tokenism," *The New York Times Magazine* (August 5, 1962), p. 11.

———, "Who Is Their God?" *The Nation*, vol. 195 (October 13, 1962), pp. 209–210.

———, "The Luminous Promise," *The Progressive*, vol. 26 (December, 1962), pp. 34ff.

———, "A Legacy of Creative Protest," *The Massachusetts Law Review*, vol. 4 (Autumn, 1962), pp. 43ff.

———, "Bold Design for a New South," *The Nation*, vol. 196 (March 30, 1963), pp. 259–262.

———, "The Ethical Demands of Integration," *Religion and Labor* (May, 1963), pp. 3ff.

———, "Emancipation — 1963," *Renewal*, vol. 3 (June, 1963), pp. 2ff.

————, "In a Word: Now," *The New York Times Magazine* (September 29, 1963), pp. 91–92.

————, "The Negro Is Your Brother," *The Atlantic Monthly*, vol. 212 (August, 1963), pp. 78–81.

————, "Hammer on Civil Rights," *The Nation*, vol. 198 (March 9, 1964), pp. 230–234.

————, "Negroes Are Not Moving Too Fast," *Saturday Evening Post* (November 7, 1964), pp. 8ff.

————, "The Acceptance" — Speech accepting the Nobel Peace Prize (December 10, 1964), in *Dear Dr. King.* New York: Buckingham Enterprises, Inc., 1968.

————, "The Lecture" — Speech delivered at Oslo University, Norway (December 11, 1964), in *Dear Dr. King.* New York: Buckingham Enterprises, Inc., 1968.

————, "Playboy Interview: Martin Luther King," *Playboy* (January, 1965), pp. 117ff.

————, "Civil Right No. 1: The Right to Vote," *The New York Times Magazine* (March 14, 1965), pp. 26–27.

————, " 'Let Justice Roll Down,' " *The Nation*, vol. 200 (March 15, 1965), pp. 269–274.

————, "Behind the Selma March," *Saturday Review*, vol. 48 (April 3, 1965), pp. 16–17.

————, "The Un-Christian Christian: SCLC Looks Closely at Christianity in a Troubled Land," *Ebony*, vol. 20 (August, 1965), pp. 76–80.

————, "Next Stop: The North," *Saturday Review*, vol. 48 (November 13, 1965), pp. 33–35.

————, "The Last Steep Ascent," *The Nation*, vol. 202 (March 14, 1966), pp. 288ff.

————, "It Is Not Enough to Condemn Black Power," *The New York Times* (July 26, 1966).

————, "Nonviolence: The Only Road to Freedom," *Ebony*, vol. 21 (October, 1966), pp. 27–30.

————, "Gift of Love," *McCall's*, vol. 94 (December, 1966), pp. 146–147.

————, "Interview: Dr. Martin Luther King, Jr.," *The New York Times* (April 2, 1967).

————, "Martin Luther King Defines Black Power," *The New York Times Magazine* (June 11, 1967), pp. 26–27.

————, "New Negro Threat: Mass Disobedience," *U.S. News and World Report*, vol. 63 (August 28, 1967), p. 10.

————, "Showdown for Non-violence," *Look*, vol. 32 (April 16, 1968), pp. 23–25.

————, "The American Dream," *The Negro History Bulletin*, vol. 31 (May, 1968), pp. 10–15.

———, "Honoring Dr. Du Bois," *Freedomways,* vol. 8 (Spring, 1968), pp. 104ff.

———, "Dark Yesterdays, Bright Tomorrows," *The Reader's Digest,* vol. 92 (June, 1968), pp. 55–58.

———, "Say That I Was a Drum Major," *The Reader's Digest,* vol. 92 (June, 1968), pp. 58–59.

———, "A Testament of Hope," *Playboy* (January, 1969), pp. 175ff.

———, "A View from the Mountaintop," *Renewal,* vol. 9 (April, 1969), pp. 3ff.

———, "A New Sense of Direction," *Worldview,* vol. 15 (April, 1972), pp. 5ff.

IV. BOOKS *about Martin Luther King Jr.*

Bartlett, Robert, "Martin Luther King, Jr.," in Robert Bartlett, *They Stand Invincible.* New York: Thomas Y. Crowell Company, 1959.

Bennett, Lerone, Jr., *What Manner of Man.* Chicago: Johnson Publishing Co.–Book Division, 1964.

Bishop, James, *The Days of Martin Luther King, Jr.* New York: G. P. Putnam's Sons, 1971.

Bleiweiss, Robert M., ed., *Marching to Freedom: The Life of Martin Luther King, Jr.* New York: The New American Library Inc., 1969.

Clayton, Edward, *The Southern Christian Leadership Conference Story.* Atlanta: SCLC, 1964.

Curtis, C. J., "The Negro Contribution to American Theology: King," *Contemporary Protestant Thought.* New York: Bruce Books, 1970.

Davis, L. G., *I Have a Dream: The Life & Times of Martin Luther King.* Chicago: Adams Press, 1969.

Griffin, John Howard, "Martin Luther King," Melville Harcourt, ed., *Thirteen for Christ.* New York: Sheed & Ward, Inc., 1963.

Holmes, Richard, "The Ordeal of Martin Luther King," Phil Hirsch, ed., *Listen, White Man, I'm Bleeding.* New York: Pyramid Books, 1969.

Illai, V., ed., *Indian Leaders on King.* New Delhi: Century Press, 1968.

King, Coretta Scott, *My Life with Martin Luther King, Jr.* New York: Holt, Rinehart & Winston, Inc., 1969.

Lewis, David L., *King: A Critical Biography.* Baltimore: Penguin Books, Inc., 1970.

Lincoln, C. Eric, ed., *Martin Luther King, Jr.: A Profile.* New York: Hill & Wang, Inc., 1970.

Lokos, Lionel, *House Divided: The Life and Legacy of Martin Luther King.* New Rochelle, N.Y.: Arlington House, Inc., 1968.

Lomax, Louis, *To Kill a Black Man* (Martin Luther King and Malcolm X). Los Angeles: Holloway House Publishing Company, 1968.

Mays, Benjamin, "Eulogy for Martin Luther King, Jr.," *Disturbed About Man.* Richmond: John Knox Press, 1969.

Miller, William Robert, *Martin Luther King, Jr.: His Life, Martyrdom and Meaning for the World.* New York: Weybright and Talley, Inc., 1968.

Muller, Gerald A., *Martin Luther King, Jr.: Civil Rights Leader.* Minneapolis: T. S. Denison, 1971.

Reddick, Lawrence D., *Crusader Without Violence: Martin Luther King, Jr.* New York: Harper & Row, Publishers, 1959.

Richardson, Herbert, "Martin Luther King, Jr.: Unsung Theologian," Martin Marty and Dean Peerman, eds., *New Theology No. 6.* New York: The Macmillan Company, 1969.

Slack, Kenneth, *Martin Luther King.* Naperville, Ill.: Alec R. Allenson, Inc., 1970.

Smith, Donald H., "Martin Luther King, Jr.: Rhetorician of Revolt." Ph.D. dissertation, University of Wisconsin, 1964.

Uwen, Nathan, *Martin Luther King, Jr.* New York: New Dimensions Publishing Company, 1970.

Walton, Hanes, Jr., *The Political Philosophy of Martin Luther King, Jr.* Westport, Conn.: Greenwood Press, Inc., 1971.

William, John A., *The King God Didn't Save: Reflections on the Life & Death of Martin Luther King.* New York: Coward, McCann & Geoghegan, Inc., 1970.

Memorial — Martin Luther King. New York: Country Wide Publications, 1968.

I Have a Dream. New York: Time-Life Books, 1968.

Martin Luther King, Jr., Nineteen Twenty-Nine to Nineteen Sixty-Eight. Chicago: Johnson Publishing Co.–Book Division, 1968.

Martin Luther King, Jr.: His Life — His Death. Fort Worth: Sepia Publishers, 1968.

V. ARTICLES *about Martin Luther King Jr.*

Ashmore, Harry S., "Martin Luther King, Spokesman for the Southern Negro," *New York Herald Tribune Book Review* (Sept. 21, 1958).

Baldwin, James, "A Dangerous Road Before Martin Luther King," *Harpers,* vol. 222 (February, 1961), pp. 33–42.

———, "Malcolm and Martin," *Esquire,* vol. 77 (April, 1972), pp. 94–97.

Bennett, Lerone, "The King Plan for Freedom," *Ebony* (July, 1956), pp. 77ff.

———, "The South and the Negro," *Ebony* (April, 1957), pp. 77ff.

———, "The Martyrdom of Martin Luther King, Jr.," *Ebony,* vol. 23 (May, 1968), pp. 174–181.

Bowles, Chester, "What Negroes Can Learn from Gandhi," *Saturday Evening Post,* vol. 230 (March 1, 1958), pp. 19–21.

Carberg, Warren, "The Story Behind the Victory," *Bostonia* (Spring, 1957), pp. 7ff.

Clark, Dennis, "Toward Equality," *Commonweal*, vol. 80 (July 24, 1964), pp. 518ff.

Clayton, Helen J., "Martin Luther King: The Right Man at the Right Time," *The YWCA Magazine* (June, 1968).

Cleghorn, Reese, "Martin Luther King, Jr., Apostle of Crisis," *Saturday Evening Post* (June 15, 1963).

Collins, L. J., "Biography of Martin Luther King," *Contemporary Review*, vol. 208 (June, 1966), pp. 362ff.

Cook, Bruce, "King in Chicago," *Commonweal*, vol. 84 (April 29, 1966), pp. 175–177.

Dunbar, Ernest, "A Visit with Dr. King," *Look* (February 12, 1963).

Elder, John Dixon, "Martin Luther King and American Civil Religion," *Harvard Divinity School Bulletin*, vol. 1 (Spring, 1968), pp. 17ff.

Fager, Charles E., "Dilemma for Dr. King," *The Christian Century*, vol. 83 (March 16, 1966), pp. 331–332.

Galphin, Bruce M., "The Political Future of Dr. King," *The Nation*, vol. 193 (September 23, 1961), pp. 177–180.

Good, Paul, "Chicago Summer: Bossism, Racism and Dr. King," *The Nation*, vol. 203 (September 19, 1966), pp. 237–242.

Griffin, John Howard, "Martin Luther King's Moment," *The Sign* (April, 1963), pp. 28ff.

Halberstam, David, "Second Coming of Martin Luther King," *Harpers*, vol. 235 (August, 1967), pp. 39–51.

———, "Notes from the Bottom of the Mountain," *Harpers*, vol. 236 (June, 1968), pp. 40–42.

Hentoff, Nat, "A Peaceful Army," *Commonweal*, vol. 72 (June 10, 1960), pp. 275–278.

King, Coretta Scott, "The Legacy of Martin Luther King, Jr.," *Theology Today*, vol. 28 (July, 1970), pp. 129ff.

Krasnow, Erwin G., "Reflections on Martin Luther King, Jr., Versus Mister Maestro," *Georgetown Law Journal*, vol. 53 (Winter, 1965), pp. 52ff.

Long, Margaret, "Martin Luther King, Jr.: 'He Kept so Plain,'" *The Progressive*, vol. 32 (May, 1968), pp. 20ff.

Lynd, Staughton, "The New Negro Radicalism," *Commentary*, vol. 36 (September, 1963), pp. 252ff.

Maguire, John David, "Martin Luther King and Viet Nam," *Christianity and Crisis*, vol. 27 (May 1, 1967), pp. 98ff.

McClendon, James William, "Martin Luther King: Politician or American Church Father?" *Journal of Ecumenical Studies*, vol. 8 (Winter, 1971), pp. 115ff.

———, "Biography as Theology," *Cross Currents*, vol. 21 (Fall, 1971), pp. 415ff.

McGraw, James R., "An Interview with Andrew J. Young," *Christianity and Crisis*, vol. 27 (January 22, 1968), pp. 324ff.

Meier, August, "On the Role of Martin Luther King," *New Politics*, vol. 4 (Winter, 1965), pp. 52ff.

Miller, Perry, "The Mind and Faith of Martin Luther King," *The Reporter Magazine*, vol. 19 (October 30, 1958), p. 40.

Miller, William Robert, "Gandhi and King: Trail Blazers in Nonviolence," *Fellowship*, vol. 35 (January, 1969), pp. 5ff.

Priven, Francis P., and Richard A. Cloward, "Dissensus Politics," *New Republic*, vol. 158 (April 20, 1968), pp. 20ff.

Quarles, Benjamin, "Martin Luther King in History," *The Negro History Bulletin*, vol. 31 (May, 1968), p. 9.

Romero, Patricia W., "Martin Luther King and His Challenge to White America," *The Negro History Bulletin*, vol. 31 (May, 1968), pp. 6–8.

Rowan, Carl T., "Heart of a Passionate Dilemma," *Saturday Review*, vol. 42 (August 1, 1959), pp. 20–21.

———, "Martin Luther King's Tragic Decision," *The Reader's Digest*, vol. 91 (September, 1967), pp. 37–42.

Schrag, Peter, "The Uses of Martyrdom," *Saturday Review*, vol. 51 (April 20, 1968), pp. 28–29.

Schulz, William, "Martin Luther King's March on Washington," *The Reader's Digest*, vol. 92 (April, 1968), pp. 65–69.

Sellers, James E., "Love, Justice and the Non-Violent Movement," *Theology Today*, vol. 18 (January, 1962), pp. 422ff.

Sitton, Claude, "Doctor King, Symbol of the Segregation Struggle," *New York Times Magazine* (January 22, 1961), p. 10.

Smith, Donald H., "An Exegesis of Martin Luther King, Jr.'s Social Philosophy," *Phylon*, vol. 31 (Spring, 1970), pp. 89ff.

Smith, Kenneth L., "Martin Luther King, Jr.: Reflections of a Former Teacher," *The Voice of Crozer Theological Seminary*, vol. 57 (April, 1965), pp. 2ff.

Smith, Lillian, "And Suddenly Something Happened," *Saturday Review*, vol. 41 (September 20, 1958), p. 21.

Smylie, James H., "On Jesus, Pharaohs, and the Chosen People: Martin Luther King as Biblical Interpreter and Humanist," *Interpretation*, vol. 24 (January, 1970), pp. 74ff.

Stackhouse, Max L., "Christianity in New Formation: Reflections of a White Christian on the Death of Dr. Martin Luther King, Jr.," *Andover Newton Quarterly* (November, 1968).

Steinkraus, Warren E., "Martin Luther King's Personalism," *Journal of the History of Ideas*, vol. 34 (Jan.–March, 1973), pp. 97–111.

Thomas, C. W., "Nobel Peace Prize Goes to Martin Luther King," *The Negro History Bulletin,* vol. 27 (November, 1964), p. 35.

Wainwright, Loudan, "Martyr of the Sit-Ins," *The Negro History Bulletin,* vol. 24 (April, 1961), pp. 147–151.

"Martin Luther King, Jr.: 'Man of 1963,' " *The Negro History Bulletin,* vol. 27 (March, 1964), pp. 136–137.

"King Speaks for Peace," *The Christian Century,* vol. 84 (April 19, 1967), pp. 492–493.

"Martin Luther King's Tropic Interlude," *Ebony,* vol. 22 (June, 1967), pp. 112–114.

"Martin Luther King, Jr. and Mahatma Gandhi," *The Negro History Bulletin,* vol. 31 (May, 1968), pp. 4–5.

"Martyrdom Comes to America's Moral Leader," *The Christian Century,* vol. 85 (April 17, 1968), p. 475.

"The Life and Death of Martin Luther King," *Christianity Today,* vol. 12 (April 26, 1968), pp. 37–40.

"The Legacy of Martin Luther King," *Life,* vol. 64 (April 19, 1968), p. 4.

"Dr. King's Legacy," *Commonweal,* vol. 88 (April 19, 1968), pp. 125–126.

"Dr. King, One Year After: He Lives, Man!" *Look,* vol. 33 (April 15, 1969), pp. 29–31.

Index